My Students' FAVORITE Chinese Recipes

updated edition

by Norma Chang

a collection of classroom-tested popular recipes

ISBN 0-9618759-4-1

Library of Congress Catalog Card No. 00-090428

Published in the United States of America by
The Travelling Gourmet
P.O. Box 911
Wappingers Falls, NY 12590

e-mail address: Luv2wok@aol.com
web address: http://members.aol.com/luv2wok/norma.htm

Manufactured in the United States of America

thanks
to
my students for encouragement
my friends for help
my family for support

TABLE OF CONTENTS

A NOTE FROM NORMA

I am still receiving requests for my cookbook, *My Students' Favorite Chinese Recipes,* which has been out of print. In response to these requests, I decided that instead of simply reprinting a cookbook I wrote more than ten years ago, I would modernize it. By bringing this cookbook up-to-date to reflect the changes in our cooking and eating habits, it will better accommodate our busy lifestyle.

This updated edition includes all the features you loved in the original plus the following:

Practical Variations: With the many demands on our limited time, it can become quite a challenge to plan and prepare the daily meals that your family will enjoy. By making minor changes to basic recipes, meals planning becomes easier. My hope is that after you have tried a few of these variations, you will create your own ideas using some of your favorite foods, and make changes to accommodate your individual tastes and needs.

Content Pages with Cross References: Each section's content page includes cross-reference guides for related recipes located in other sections of the book. This feature will make locating a recipe easier.

Ingredients List in both English and Chinese for shopping convenience.

As in the original version, even more *do-ahead instructions, substitutions, kitchen hints* and *time saving tips* are sprinkled throughout the book to help make kitchen tasks more efficient and life in the kitchen more fun. The unique layout and grouping of ingredients make the recipes easier to understand and execute, enabling you to get meals to the table faster without impacting the integrity of the finished dish.

I hope you enjoy these recipes as much as my students do. Many of them discovered that when short on time, stir-frying is the quickest way to get healthy, delicious meals on the table. They also discovered that a wok in not a must when stir-frying. A frying pan, Dutch oven or any pot that you already have in your kitchen will do a good stir-frying job.

Eat slowly! Remember to take time to savor the food you prepared.

Norma Chang

EQUIPMENT

WOKS come in different sizes and shapes and are made from a variety of material. Electric and non-electric.

There is the traditional round-bottom wok, most suitable for gas ranges. Then there is the flat-bottom wok which many people prefer for use on an electric range.

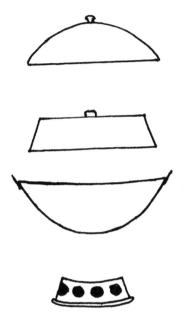

For most household use, a 14-inch diameter wok is the most practical size. I prefer a cast iron or carbon steel wok. Cast iron and carbon steel appliances are much better heat conductors and these appliances perform better the more they are used. I also prefer the traditional round bottom wok to a flat bottom wok even on an electric range.

Whether to select a wok with the traditional two metal loops or with two metal loops covered with wood or with one metal loop and a long wooden handle is strictly a personal preference. If selecting a wok with a long wooden handle, place it on a flat surface to test whether the wok is balanced or not.

Personally, I do not use a wok ring. I prefer to set my wok directly on the electrical element of my range. But for safety reason, when steaming or deep frying in a wok on the range, do use a wok ring. If your wok ring is a tapered one, have the wide side up on an electric range and the narrow side up on a gas range.

Your brand new carbon steel, spun steel or cast iron wok is covered with a coating of industrial oil to prevent rusting. Before use, wash wok inside and outside thoroughly with cleanser to remove all traces of industrial oil. Dry wok with paper towels. If paper towel discolors, repeat the washing and drying. Place dried wok on range. Heat at low until the whole wok is heated through, about 15 minutes. Using a paper towel, wipe a thin layer of vegetable oil onto the INSIDE of the wok. Heat on low for another 15 minutes. Turn off range, leave wok on the range to cool. Your wok is now ready to use.

EQUIPMENT (continued)

Wash wok immediately after each use with warm water and a sponge, add a little soap, if needed. Dry thoroughly. Repeat the oiling process. Gradually your wok will begin to develop a patina on the INSIDE surface (a smooth dark surface, not to be confused with burned on food.) The patina will first appear at the inside lower portion of the wok gradually spreading to the entire inside surface. This patina is what we want to acquire so DO NOT scrub it off.

Cooking tomatoes and other acidic food in your seasoned wok will remove some of the patina. Do not panic, this lost patina will be re-acquired after one or two uses.

Once your wok has developed a patina wash IMMEDIATELY, after each use, while it is still hot and dry thoroughly. There is no need to oil.

When a carbon steel or spun steel wok is new, it reflects heat. The first few times you use your new wok, you will feel a lot of heat radiating onto you. As the wok is used, the OUTSIDE surface will blacken (first the lower portion, gradually spreading to the entire outside surface of the wok) thus absorbing the heat from the range instead of reflecting it. The better a wok is seasoned, the faster the food will cook and you will feel less heat radiating onto you. The seasoning process takes a little time and patience, but gets there eventually.

Select a high-dome wok cover or a high-flat wok cover. The cover should be about one inch smaller in diameter that the wok.

KITCHEN HINT: To get more use from your carbon steel wok, take it to the backyard cookout. Set it directly on the grill and stir-fry sway.

KITCHEN HINT: To remove rust from your wok, wash with vinegar. The rust will disappear before your eyes. Rinse with water, dry and wipe with a lightly oiled paper towel.

CHINESE SPATULA, also called a turner,
is not necessary but it works well with the wok. It is made of metal with a short wooden handle and is shaped like a shovel. The shape makes it easy to stir-fry in the wok. The size I use, in my 14-inch wok, is made of stainless steel, about 4 inches wide with a 10-inch long handle.

EQUIPMENT (continued)

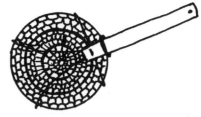

CHINESE STRAINER also called a mesh spoon, is made of copper or stainless steel wire with a bamboo handle. It is used to remove food from hot oil or hot water. The 7-inch diameter size is the most useful.

The bamboo handle can serve as a thermometer when deep frying without the aid of a temperature controlled appliance. Place your strainer in the hot oil. When fast bubbles appear around the bamboo handle in the hot oil, the oil temperature is about 375 degrees, the right temperature for deep frying.

The Chinese strainer is also useful for removing vegetables and other foods from blanching water.

CHINESE SCISSORS shape remains the same whether they are the small embroidery scissors or the large tailor scissors.

Its symmetrical shape also makes it versatile. The same scissors can be used by either a right-handed person or a left-handed person.

I find the 4¾-inch size the ideal kitchen scissors, especially for deveining shrimp. Shelling and deveining is done in one operation. It is also handy for snipping herbs and many other small kitchen tasks.

Made of steel, the Chinese scissors maintain a beautiful sharp edge that never seems to dull. They will rust, so do wash and dry immediately after each use and it will last, it seems, forever.

Deveining Shrimp with the Chinese Scissors

❶ Cut through the shell and the shrimp meat (just below the shell where the vein is, no need to cut deeper) from the head-end to the tail.

❷ Remove and discard shell and vein. Rinse shrimp and pat dry.

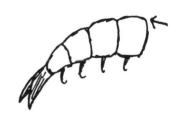

EQUIPMENT (continued)

CHINESE CLEAVER is very versatile.
Once you are used to a cleaver, you will
wonder how you ever got along without one.

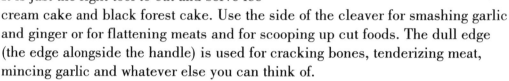

Besides slicing, shredding, mincing and
chopping, use your cleaver as a cake server.
It is just the right tool to cut and serve ice
cream cake and black forest cake. Use the side of the cleaver for smashing garlic
and ginger or for flattening meats and for scooping up cut foods. The dull edge
(the edge alongside the handle) is used for cracking bones, tenderizing meat,
mincing garlic and whatever else you can think of.

The most practical cleaver for household use is the all-purpose cleaver (No.3)
This is heavier than a slicing cleaver and can be used to cut through poultry
bones, but not spareribs.

Get into the habit of washing and drying your cleaver after each use. NEVER put
your cleaver in the dish washer especially if it has a wooden handle.

Sharpening the cleaver
A sharp knife not only makes the job of cutting faster and easier, a sharp knife is
also safer to use. A dull knife requires more pressure when cutting, therefore
increasing the chances of the knife slipping.

You may wish to have your cleaver sharpened professionally. However, the job
can be accomplished satisfactorily at home using a sharpening stone (also called
a whet stone.)

A sharpening stone is a flat stone that works on the same principle as a nail file.
It has two sides, one coarse the other fine. Sharpening stones come in various
sizes. The 7-x2-x1-inch size is adequate for most household uses.

To sharpen your cleaver:
❶ Wet the sharpening stone. Place it on a
   flat surface, coarse side up.
❷ Wet the cleaver. With right hand holding
   the cleaver handle, and the cutting edge
   to the left, place the cutting edge at a 15-
   degree angle on the stone. Rest the left

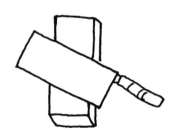

EQUIPMENT (continued)

hand on top of the blade to keep the cleaver steady and to maintain the 15-degree angle.

❸ Move the cutting edge back and forth on the stone for about 10 - 20 times, depending on how dull the cleaver is, keeping the stone wet all the time.

❹ Reverse the process, left hand holding the cleaver handle, cutting edge to the right, right hand on top of blade, sharpen the other side of the blade.

❺ For a sharper and smoother finish, turn the stone over, fine side up, repeat the whole process, 5 - 10 passes on each side of the cutting edge.

❻ Wash the stone before storing. Wash the cleaver before using.

BAMBOO STEAMERS are round steamer baskets constructed of either all bamboo or a combination of bamboo slats and wooden side. For most household uses, two tiers and a cover are adequate. The 12-inch diameter size is the most practical. This size will fit perfectly in a 14-inch wok, or you may choose to place the steamer baskets on top of a stockpot that is a perfect fit.

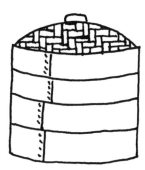

When buying bamboo steamers make sure the tiers and cover fit snugly into each other.

Before using your new bamboo steamer, immerse it in water for 2 - 3 hours to break it in. Rinse thoroughly with warm water. Steamer is now ready to use.

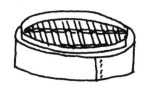

After each use, wash well with hot water. DO NOT use detergent. Air dry thoroughly (to prevent mildew) before storing, unwrapped, in a dry place away from direct sunlight.

Because the woven bamboo lid absorbs the steaming moisture and the excess moisture is able to escape through the weaves, condensation problems associated with metal steamers are avoided when using bamboo steamers. They are, however, a bit of a challenge to maintain. I clean the bamboo slots with a stiff toothbrush dedicated for this purpose.

EQUIPMENT (continued)

METAL STEAMER consists of a base, which sits directly on the range, 2 or 3 perforated tiers and a cover. Various sizes are available. Select the size best suited for your needs.

When buying a metal steamer, make sure the base, tiers and cover fit snugly into each other and the perforated part is sturdy. If possible, select one with a dome cover instead of a flat cover.

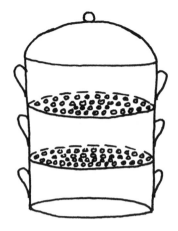

STEAMER RACK is a round, sturdy, perforated "pizza pan." The 12-inch diameter rack is the best size for a 14-inch wok. It is not necessary if you already own a metal or bamboo steamer.

FONDUE STRAINER also called a fondue basket is a little mesh basket, 2½-inch in diameter with a 6-inch wire handle. It is made of copper or stainless steel wire.

CUTTING TECHNIQUES

SLICING: This is cutting meat, poultry, seafood or vegetables into slices, the thickness depending on your need and preference.

SHREDDING: Neatly stack a few slices of the sliced food, then cut lengthwise into strips of the same thickness as the slices. The thinner the slices the thinner the strips, the thicker the slices the thicker the strips.

DICING: Cut the shredded strips of food into cubes. The thinner the slices, the thinner the strips and the smaller the cubed pieces. The thicker the slices, the thicker the strips and the larger the cubed pieces.

MINCING: Chop the diced food with the cleaver or a knife until it reaches the desired texture.

SLANT CUT: Hold the cleaver at an angle to the food being cut. The smaller the angle, the larger the pieces of cut food. The larger the angle, the smaller the pieces of cut food.

ROLL CUT: Cut off a piece of food at about a 45-degree angle. Make a ¼ or a ⅓ turn if the remaining piece of uncut food, Cut at a 45-degree angle. Repeat until the whole piece of food is cut. You will end up with irregular shaped pieces of food that have more exposed surface for faster cooking.

COOKING TECHNIQUES

STIR-FRYING is cooking food, with a little oil, on top of the range using high heat. Stir and toss the food until the desired doneness is reached. Stir-frying is a very fast cooking process. It is, therefore, very wise to have everything ready and within easy reach before proceeding.

A wok is ideal for this task but not necessary. You can stir-fry in a shallow pot, such as a Dutch oven, or a frying pan. I prefer a Dutch oven over a frying pan. (Because the side of the Dutch oven is higher than a frying pan, there is less spattering onto the stove and other areas during cooking and so there is less cleaning to do.) The disadvantage of using a pot or frying pan is that more oil is needed because of the larger cooking surface to be covered by the oil.

Preheat your appliance (wok, pot or frying pan) slowly and thoroughly before adding room temperature oil. Food cooked in a properly preheated appliance will not stick, not even scrambled eggs.

Before I begin preparing the food I am going to stir-fry, I set my wok on the range and turn it to the lowest setting. That way when I have finished all my preparations, my wok is thoroughly heated through. I then add room temperature oil to the wok and turn the range to the desired temperature setting. When the desired temperature is reached, I proceed to stir-fry.

A point to remember when stir-frying in a wok is that the lower portion of the wok is the hottest. So as you stir-fry, if you discover some pieces of food are cooked and others not quite done, just move the cooked pieces to the upper portion of the wok, and the not-quite-done pieces to the lower portion.

Also, if the heat on an electric range appears too hot, rather than lowering the temperature, lift the wok off the range for a few seconds. This will lower the temperature in the wok sufficiently to resume cooking.

DEEP-FRYING is cooking food in very hot oil. Properly prepared deep-fried food is not at all greasy. Corn, peanut, canola or soybean oil is suitable for deep frying. Olive oil or olive oil combination is unsuitable due to its low smoking point. Food to be deep fried, ideally, should be at room temperature.

Oil can be re-used if it looks clean and smells fresh. Cool the hot oil and strain through double thicknesses of cheesecloth, coffee filter or fine-mesh strainer.

COOKING TECHNIQUES (continued)

To deep-fry:
❶ Heat wok or pot. Add room temperature oil and heat to desired temperature.

❷ Add food a few pieces at a time. Too many pieces of food at one time will lower the oil temperature causing the deep-fried food to taste greasy.

❸ Cook food to desired doneness, remove with a Chinese strainer or a slotted spoon, drain on paper towels.

KITCHEN HINT: Lacking a thermostatically controlled appliance when deep frying? Use the following methods.

(1) Drop a piece of food in the hot oil. If the food sinks and bubbles, then floats to the surface, the oil temperature is about 350°. If the food floats to the surface at once, the oil temperature is about 375°.

OR (2) Place a Chinese strainer (the bamboo part must touch the oil), a bamboo chopstick or a wooden spoon in the hot oil. If fast bubbles appear around the bamboo or wooden parts, the oil temperature is about 375°.

STEAMING is cooking food with moist heat. Food to be steamed can be placed directly on the steamer rack, lined (with a damp, clean steamer cloth or cheesecloth or with a vegetable) or unlined, on a heatproof plate or in a heatproof bowl. Make sure the plate or bowl used is at least ½ inch smaller (all around) than the steamer tier to allow free movement of the steam. Remember the steam must reach the food to cook it.

Water in the steamer base should not touch the food being steamed. The surface of the water should be at least 1 inch, preferably 2 inches, away from the bottom of the steamer rack or the dish being used.

If the steamer base cannot hold sufficient water to cook the food for the required time, have a kettle of boiling water ready to replenish when water level gets low. You will, however, need to increase the cooking time by a few minutes each time you open the steamer.

To steam:
❶ Add water to steamer base (this can be a wok, pot, frying pan or the base that comes with a steamer set) and bring to boil using high heat.

❷ Place food in steamer basket or on steamer rack.

❸ Cover. Steam as per recipe's instructions.

GINGER WINE

Ginger and wine are two ingredients called for in most of my recipes. Ginger is highly perishable and it always gets lost among the various vegetables in my refrigerator. To save time and money, I decided to combine ginger and wine in a glass jar with a tight-fitting, non-corrosive lid. Stored on the refrigerator door shelf, I know exactly where to find ginger and wine whenever I need them.

fresh ginger
pale dry sherry, sake or rice wine

(1) Peel ginger. Wash, pat dry and slice thinly.
(2) Place sliced ginger in a glass jar (or other non-corrosive container) with a tight-fitting, non-corrosive lid. Cover with sherry, sake or rice wine. Will keep up to 6 months in the refrigerator.

NOTE:	Cooking sherry and rice wine sold at the supermarkets and Asian food markets contain salt. Check the label.
KITCHEN HINT:	Ran out of ginger wine? Not to worry. Just add the amount of wine called for in the recipe and a few slices of fresh ginger.
GRATING GINGER:	Use a ginger grater, available at Asian markets. Or cover a fine grater with a piece of plastic wrap. Peel and grate ginger. Lift up plastic wrap. Scrape off grated ginger and use as needed.
EXTRACTING GINGER JUICE:	Pulverize a chunk of peeled ginger, using a mortar and pestle. If you don't have that equipment, smash a chunk of ginger with the flat side of your cleaver, place the smashed ginger in a cup or bowl, and use the handle of your cleaver to finish the pulverizing job. Add 1 - 2 teaspoons of water or pale dry sherry to the pulverized ginger. Work the mixture with your fingers to release all the ginger oil and flavor. Squeeze out as much of the liquid as possible. Strain if desired.
USING GINGER FROM GINGER WINE:	☞ Add a few slices to the stockpot when making broth.
	☞ Add a few slices to stew.
	☞ Add 1, 2 or more slices to the oil when stir-frying vegetables.
	☞ Put some at the bottom of the roasting pan when making a roast.
	☞ Place a few slices in the cavity of a whole chicken before roasting.

APPETIZERS

BEEF SATAY

makes 15 - 24

1 pound flank, sirloin flap steak or *chuck top blade* Cut across the grain
into about ¼-inch thick, long slices.

1 tablespoon sugar	)
2 tablespoons ginger wine, p. 16	) Combine. Add beef.
1 tablespoon dark or mushroom soy sauce	) Mix to coat each
1 - 2 tablespoons oil	) slice evenly.
1 teaspoon cornstarch	) Can be done the
1 - 3 tablespoons Bull Head barbecue sauce	) day before and
½ teaspoon kosher salt or to taste	) refrigerated.
1 - 2 cloves garlic Finely minced	)

15 - 24 8-inch bamboo skewers Soak in water 30 minutes before using.
15 - 24 cherry tomatoes

(1) Thread 1 or 2 slices of beef, accordion style, onto each bamboo skewer. This
can be done ahead of time and refrigerated.
(2) Place skewered beef, single layer, on lightly oiled broiler grid or on a baking
rack set over a roasting pan. Broil about 3 inches from heat source, for 5
minutes. Turn, broil 2 - 5 minutes or until reached desired doneness.
(3) Place a cherry tomato at tip of skewer. Serve hot or cold.

****

Practical Variations

CHICKEN SATAY
Substitute: *1 pound boneless and skinless chicken breast* for the *beef*

PORK SATAY
Substitute: *1 pound lean boneless pork sirloin* for the *beef*

LAMB SATAY
Substitute: *1 pound boneless leg of lamb* for the *beef*

TOFU SATAY
Substitute: *1 pound extra firm tofu* for the *beef* Drain tofu. Wrap in a thick
clean kitchen towel. Refrigerate 2 hours preferably overnight. Cut
this super firm tofu into about ½-inch thick slices.

My Students' Favorite Chinese Recipes, updated edition

CURRIED BEEF STRIPS

makes 15 - 24

1 pound flank steak, chuck top blade, sirloin flap or sirloin steak Cut across the grain into about ¼-inch thick long slices.

2 cloves garlic Finely minced	)
1 tablespoon cornstarch	) Combine. This is the marinade.
1 - 2 tablespoons curry powder	) Add beef slices. Mix well.
1 tablespoon ginger wine, p. 16	) Marinate ½ hour if time
1 tablespoon regular soy sauce	) permits. Can be done the day
1 tablespoon oil	) before and refrigerated. More
½ teaspoon kosher salt or to taste	) flavorful prepared day before.
1½ teaspoons brown sugar	)

15 - 24 bamboo skewers (8-inch) Soak in water at least 30 minutes.
3 - 4 small zucchini Cut into about 15 - 24 ¾-inch thick pieces

(1) Thread 1 or 2 slices of beef, accordion style, onto each bamboo skewer. Place 1 piece of zucchini at the tip of the skewer. This can be done the day before and refrigerated.
(2) Place, single layer, on lightly oiled broiler grid or on a rack set over a roasting pan.
(3) Broil, on high, about 3 inches from heat source for 4 - 5 minutes on each side or until reached desired doneness.

****

Practical Variations

SOUTHEAST ASIA CURRIED BEEF STRIPS

Substitute: *1 - 2 tablespoons fish sauce* for the *regular soy sauce*
Add to marinade: *¼ - ½ cup unsweetened coconut milk*
                 minced fresh chilies or *Asian chili sauce* to taste

CURRIED SHRIMP KABOBS

Substitute: *1¼ pound large shrimp* for the *beef* Shell and devein shrimp.
Add: *1 each red, green and yellow peppers* Cut into about 1" x 1" pieces. Alternate shrimp and peppers on skewer, leaving about a ¼-inch space between the pieces to ensure even cooking. Broil 5 - 6 minutes on each side or until reached desired doneness.

FRIED WONTONS

½ pound lean ground pork	) Combine
¼ cup coarsely chopped water chestnuts	) well in a
1 scallion Thinly sliced	) bowl. This
3 - 5 dried Chinese mushrooms Soak at least ½ hour to)	is the won-
soften. Squeeze out excess water, remove and discard	) tons filling.
stems. Finely chop caps (about 3 tablespoons).	) Can be
½ teaspoon kosher salt or to taste	) done a day
2 teaspoons ginger wine, p.16	) ahead and
2 teaspoons regular soy sauce	) refrigerated.

¾ - 1 pound ready-made wonton wrappers (about 60)
Oil for deep frying

2 tablespoons ketchup	)
1 teaspoon Asian sesame oil	) Combine in a small serving dish.
¼ - 1 teaspoon Asian chili	) This is the sauce.
sauce or to taste (optional)	)

(1) Assemble wontons according to instructions on page 21. Place on a dry plate. Cover with a clean, damp kitchen towel.

(2) Deep fry in 375° preheated oil until golden, about 2 minutes. Drain on paper towels. Serve warm or at room temperature, with or without sauce.

****

Practical Variations

SEAFOOD FRIED WONTONS

Substitute: *½ pound sea scallops, lobster meat, crab meat* or *shrimp* (or a combination) for the *pork*
                bamboo shoots for the *water chestnuts*

DUCK FRIED WONTONS

Substitute: *½ pound minced duck meat* for the *pork*
                2 - 3 tablespoons thinly sliced Chinese chives for the *scallion*

CHICKEN FRIED WONTONS

Substitute: *½ pound ground chicken* for the *pork*

FRIED WONTONS (continued)

KITCHEN HINT: Fried wontons can be frozen and reheated. It will not, however, be as good as freshly made, but passable.

To reheat: Arrange thawed fried wontons, single layer, on a baking rack in a shallow baking pan. Bake 5 minutes in a 400° preheated oven, turning once. Fried wontons can be made the day before and refrigerated. To reheat, follow instructions above.

KITCHEN HINT: When deep frying the wontons, first put 2 or 3 wontons in the preheated oil. When the oil returns to the proper temperature, add wontons one by one so as to maintain the proper oil temperature. Do not crowd. Remove individually as each becomes golden.

How to assemble Fried Wontons:

❶ Moisten 2 adjoining edges of the wonton wrapper with water.

❷ Place about ½ teaspoon filling in the center of wrapper.

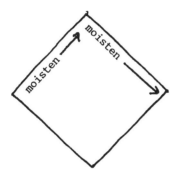

❸ Fold wrapper over to form a triangle.

❹ With thumbs and forefingers holding the 2 corners of the base, pull down and overlap. Press to seal.

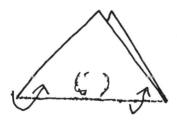

CORAL SHRIMP

1 pound large raw shrimp in shell Cut through shell on back. Remove vein but leave shell on. Snip off legs. Washed. Pat dry. **1½ teaspoons kosher salt**	)) Toss well. Refrig-) erate ½ - 2 hours.)

4 tablespoons oil
4 slices ginger
2 scallions Thinly sliced
2 - 4 cloves garlic Minced

1 tablespoon ginger wine, p. 16 **3 tablespoons ketchup** **1 teaspoon sugar**	) Combine in a small bowl.) This is the sauce.)

(1) Heat wok. Add oil, swirl to coat wok. Heat on high until reached smoking point. Add shrimp. Stir-fry over high heat until color changes and shrimp is nearly done. Remove shrimp to a plate, leaving in wok as much oil as possible.

(2) Remove all but 1 tablespoon of oil from wok. Add ginger, scallion and garlic. Stir-fry over high to medium-high heat until fragrant, about 1 - 2 minutes. Stir in the sauce. Add shrimp. Stir-fry until shrimp is cooked. Serve at once.

NOTE: This is a somewhat messy dish to eat. Since each diner must peel his/her own shrimp at the table, have extra paper napkins on hand. The sweet delicate flavor and fine texture of the shrimp cooked this way, however, makes the mess worthwhile. If you really can't stand the mess, see page 159 for alternative cooking method.

****

Practical Variation

FIERY CORAL SHRIMP

Add: **1 - 3 fresh green** or **red chili peppers**, minced, during step (2).

SHRIMP TOAST

½ pound raw shrimp Shelled. Deveined. Finely minced.	) Combine.
	) Mix very well.
1 egg white	) ***Short cut:*** Place
1 tablespoon cornstarch	) all ingredients
1 tablespoon ginger wine, p. 16	) (unminced) in
2 tablespoons finely minced water chestnuts	) food processor.
1 tablespoon finely minced pork fat (optional)	) Pulse until very
¼ teaspoon kosher salt or to taste	) fine.

8 slices 1- or 2-day old thin white bread Trim crust. Cut each slice into 4 squares or 4 triangles.

Chinese parsley or *regular parsley* (optional)

black sesame seeds or *poppy seeds* (optional)

oil for deep frying

(1) Spread about ¼-inch thickness of shrimp mixture evenly on one side of bread.

(2) Press a parsley leaf into shrimp mixture. Sprinkle on a few sesame seeds or poppy seeds, press lightly to adhere. Up to this point can be done ahead of time. Cover with plastic wrap and refrigerate.

(3) Deep fry, shrimp side down, in 375° preheated oil. When bread edges begin to brown (about 1 minute) turn and fry another 30 seconds or until golden. Drain and serve at once.

****

Practical Variations

SCALLOPS BAGUETTES

Substitute: *5 - 6 ounces sea scallops* for the *shrimp*
French baguettes for the *white bread* Cut baguettes on the diagonal into about ½-inch thick slices. Do not trim crust.

CHICKEN TOAST

Substitute: *5 - 6 ounces chicken meat* for the *shrimp*
Add: *¼ - 1 teaspoon finely minced fresh chili pepper or to taste*

SPRING ROLL

makes 15 - 20

15 - 20 spring roll skins
4 ounces roast pork (*Chinese or otherwise*) or **ham** Shredded

4 ounces raw shrimp Shelled. Deveined.)	
Coarsely chopped.)	
¼ teaspoon kosher salt or to taste)	Combine.
dash of black or white pepper or to taste)	
½ teaspoon cornstarch)	

1 cup peeled and shredded carrots
1 - 1½ cups shredded cabbage
1 8-ounce can shredded bamboo shoots Drained. Cut into shorter lengths.
2 scallions Thinly sliced
2 - 3 tablespoons oil
1 teaspoon kosher salt or to taste
½ - 1 teaspoon sugar
1 egg Lightly beaten
oil for deep frying

2 teaspoons cornstarch) Combine in a small bowl.	
1 tablespoon water) Stir well just before adding to wok.	

(1) Heat wok. Add 1 - 2 tablespoons oil. Swirl to coat wok. Add shrimp. Stir-fry over medium high to high heat until shrimp turns color. Add roast pork. Stir-fry until shrimp is cooked and pork is heated, about 2 minutes. Remove.

(2) Add 1 tablespoon oil to wok. Add salt and vegetables. Mix well. Add sugar. Stir-fry until vegetables are just under desired doneness, about 2 minutes. Add pork and shrimp. Mix well. Stir in cornstarch mixture. Mix well.

(3) Spread mixture on a platter to cool. Up to this point can be done the day before and refrigerated.

(4) Assemble spring rolls according to instructions on page 25.

(5) Deep fry in 375° preheated oil until golden, about 3 minutes. Serve warm or at room temperature.

****

Practical Variations

TURKEY SPRING ROLLS (*great way to enjoy some of the precooked Thanksgiving turkey*)
Substitute: **6 - 8 ounces roast turkey** for the **roast pork** and **shrimp**
　　　　　　4 - 6 dried Chinese mushrooms for the **bamboo shoots** Soak at least ½ hour to soften. Squeeze dry. Discard stems. Shred caps.

Practical Variations (continued)

TORTILLA ROLLS

Substitute: ***Small flour tortilla*** for the ***spring roll skin*** Wrap tortillas in foil. Warm in 300° preheated oven for 10 minutes to soften. Assemble (see below.) Place on baking pan, seam side down. Brush with butter or olive oil. Bake in a 400° preheated oven for about 10 minutes or until crisp. Skip step (5) on page 24.

PITA POCKETS

Substitute: ***Small pita halves*** for the ***spring roll skin*** Steam pita halves as per page 149. Fill with hot pork mixture and enjoy. Skip steps (3), (4) & (5) on page 24.

How to assemble Spring Rolls:

❶ Place about 2 TBS filling on 1 edge of the wrapper. Form filling into a sausage shape.

❷ Fold over edge with filling ¼.

❸ Fold over another ¼.

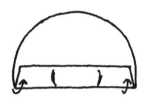

❹ Fold left and right sides toward center.

❺ Fold over another ¼. Brush remaining edge with beaten egg.

❻ Fold over the last ¼.

BARBECUED SPARERIBS

serves 6 - 8 as appetizer

2½ - 3 pounds meaty spareribs

½ teaspoon 5-spice powder	)
1½ teaspoons kosher salt or to taste	) Combine. Rub well all over
3 tablespoons sugar	) spareribs. Marinate at least
2 tablespoons ginger wine, p. 16	) 2 hours, preferably over-
2 tablespoons regular soy sauce	) night, in the refrigerator.
3 tablespoons hoisin sauce	) For more flavorful spareribs
1 square (about 1 tablespoon)	) marinate up to 2 days.
red bean curd (optional)	) Turning once or twice.
5 cloves garlic Finely minced	)

honey For basting

(1) Preheat oven to 450°. Place ribs, meat side down, on lightly oiled broiler grid or on a rack set over a roasting pan. Brush with honey. Bake in middle of oven for 15 minutes.

(2) Remove pan with ribs from oven. Pour ½ cup hot water in bottom of pan.

(3) Turn ribs, meat side up. Brush with honey. Bake another 15 - 20 minutes. Cut into individual ribs. Serve hot or at room temperature.

NOTE: *Country-style ribs* or *southern-style ribs* work well with this recipe.

KITCHEN HINT: For sweeter ribs, brush each side with honey twice.
KITCHEN HINT: For ease of cleaning, line pan with heavy duty aluminum foil.
Marinate ribs in plastic bag for ease of turning and there is no container to wash.

****

Practical Variations

CHINESE ROAST PORK

Substitute: **Boneless pork shoulder** for the **spareribs** Cut pork shoulder into 1½- to 2-inch wide strips. Leave space between each strip when baking.

BARBECUED CHICKEN

Substitute: **Chicken legs** for the **spareribs** Grill 35 - 45 minutes or until cooked or bake in 350° preheated oven 30 - 45 minutes or until tender.

DIM SUM

The end of this chapter is an appropriate place to introduce "Dim Sum", the famous Cantonese specialty. Dim sum (literal translation means "to touch the heart"), the traditional food in the Chinese teahouse, is now widely available in many Chinese restaurants.

Dim sum is a collection of mostly bite-size food eaten before 1:00 or 2:00 p.m. It can serve as breakfast, lunch or brunch. The beverage that goes with dim sum is tea. So if you are invited to "yum cha" (this means to drink tea in the Cantonese dialect), you are invited to have dim sum.

The variety of foods served during dim sum are numerous. There are all kinds of dumplings, buns, tofu (bean curd), rice, noodles, congee (thick rice soup), sweet pastries, etc. These may be steamed, deep fried, pan fried or baked. Dim sum items are served in small steamer baskets or on plates of different sizes.

All the dim sum items are delicious, and you will want to try everything. It is, therefore, best to go "yum cha" with a group of friends. This way you get to sample a greater variety of foods. Never take more than a sample of each kind, otherwise you will not have room for all the different dishes that pass by.

When you go to a restaurant for dim sum and after you are seated, a pot of hot tea and a card will be placed on your table. At some restaurants you can order special blend of teas. Feel free to ask for recommendations. The card is to keep track of the items you selected.

Carts with different kinds of food will be wheeled by. Look over the carts, if you like something that is on the cart, ask for it. If you do not recognize the items on the cart, ask, the waiter or waitress will be happy to assist you. If you do not see anything you like, drink your tea, relax, visit with your friends and wait for the next cart to come by. If you missed an item, not to worry, the cart will come around again.

Both sweet and savory items will appear simultaneously. You select and eat, as much or as little as you wish. When you select an item from a cart, the waiter or waitress will stamp the appropriate space on your card. At the end of your meal, the manager will tally up the stamps on your card and hand you the bill.

Besides the items on the carts, at some restaurants you may also order various kinds of noodle dishes from a menu. Some restaurants also have a cooking station in the dining area. Bubbling away may be shell fish, meatballs, egg-

DIM SUM (continued)

plants, etc. Bring your card with you to the cooking station and order what you like to take back to your table. The person at the cooking station will stamp your card in the appropriate space.

Some of the dim sum items are: (*Use the pronunciation of the item as a guide, not the spelling. The same item could be spelled differently at different restaurants.*)

Baked Pork Bun	A baked yeast dough with roast pork filling.
Beef Shiao Mai	Steamed beef balls.
Coconut Bar	Made from gelatin and coconut milk.
Curry Beef Patty	A semi-flaky pastry with a curried beef filling.
Fun Kuo	Mixture of meat and vegetables in a dough, can be steamed or fried.
Har Kow	Shrimp and bamboo shoots wrapped in a pleated white translucent dough and steamed.
Lo Mai Kai	Rice and chicken wrapped in lotus leaf and steamed.
Lotus Seed Bun	A steamed yeast dough with sweet lotus seed filling.
Mini Spring Roll	Meat and vegetables wrapped in a very thin dough and deep fried.
Pot Sticker Dumpling	A dough made of flour and water with a pork and vegetable filling. Pan fried.
Roast Pork Patty	A semi-flaky pastry with a Chinese roast pork filling.
Sesame Rice Dumpling	Made from glutinous rice flour with a sweet bean filling. Coated with sesame seeds. Deep fried.
Shiao Mai	Ground pork wrapped in a thin dough and steamed.
Shrimp Toast	Finely minced shrimp mixture on bread. Deep fried.
Silver Noodles	Round rice noodles stir-fried with meat and vegetables.
Steamed Pork Bun	A steamed yeast dough with roast pork filling.
Steamed Glutinous Rice	Glutinous rice mixed with vegetables and meat then steamed.
Stuffed Bean Curd	Fresh tofu stuffed with a meat and shrimp mixture. May be steamed, braised or deep fried.
Turnip Cake	Chinese turnip (daikon), pork, dried shrimp, rice flour, etc. are combined and steamed to form a cake. The cooled cake is sliced and pan fried.
Water chestnut Cake	Water chestnut flour, sugar and water combined and steamed to form a cake. The cooled cake is sliced and pan fried.

SOUP

HOMEMADE BROTH

makes about 6 cups

2 - 2½ pounds fresh chicken bones with some meat on
1 scallion Cleaned. Leave whole or cut into 2 or 3 sections.
2 - 3 slices fresh ginger
1 carrot Cut into chunks or slices
2 teaspoons kosher salt or to taste
cold water to cover bones about 1 inch (9 - 10 cups)

(1) Place all of the above in a large pot. Bring to a boil, using high heat, uncovered. Remove and discard any scum that appears on the surface.

(2) Lower heat to maintain a slow simmer. Cover. Simmer about 3 hours. DO NOT stir during this simmering period (stirring will result in cloudy broth.)

(3) Strain broth through a fine strainer. Add salt to taste. Use as directed in recipes.

NOTE: This is a basic recipe. Tailor it to your individual tastes by adding other ingredients. Examples: tomato, lemon juice, lemongrass, celery, Chinese red dates, peppercorns, parsley, etc.

KITCHEN HINT: For a richer broth, substitute part of the chicken bones with pork bones. Cook the same way.

KITCHEN HINT: Freeze cooled broth in ice cube trays. Once frozen, remove from ice cube tray. Store in freezer bags or freezer containers. Label, date and return to freezer. Use as needed. Will keep up to 6 months. Make a note of how many table-spoons of liquid each broth cube contains.
For individual servings, freeze cooled broth in muffin pans. Once frozen, remove from muffin pan. Store in freezer bags or freezer containers. Label, date and return to freezer.

****

Practical Variation

HOMEMADE BROTH 2

❶ Brown scallion and ginger in 1 tablespoon oil.

❷ Add bones and brown, all sides, lightly.

❸ Add water. Bring to a boil, using high heat, uncovered. Remove and discard any scum that appears on the surface.

❹ Continue with steps (2) and (3) of Homemade Broth above.

30 Soup   My Students' Favorite Chinese Recipes, updated edition

CHINESE NOODLES SOUP serves 3 - 4

½ pound fresh Chinese noodles Parboil 5 - 7 minutes. Drain. Cool under
   cold running water. Drain again well. Cut into shorter lengths.

2 - 4 ounces Chinese roast pork, ham or ***other cooked meat*** Thinly sliced.

4 ounces raw shrimp Shelled (leave
    tail on) Deveined. Washed. Pat dry.
    Butterfly, p 35.
 ¼ teaspoon kosher salt
 2 slices fresh ginger
	)
	)
	) Combine.
	)
	)

2 - 4 ounces snowpeas Stringed
½ - 1 carrot Peeled. Thinly sliced.
8 or more small mushrooms Leave whole or cut in 2 or 3
1 scallion Thinly sliced or shredded.
4 - 6 cups chicken broth
Asian sesame oil (optional)
Asian chili oil or ***Asian chili sauce*** (optional)

(1) In a large pot, bring broth to boil. Add shrimp. Cook until color changes and
   shrimp is cooked. Remove with a slotted spoon and set aside.
(2) Add snowpeas, carrot and mushrooms to broth. Bring to boil. Cook until
   vegetables reach desired doneness. Remove with slotted spoon and set aside.
(3) Add noodles to broth. Bring to boil. Ladle noodles and broth into individual
   soup bowls. Top with cooked meat, shrimp, vegetables and scallion. Add a
   few drops of sesame oil and or chili oil/chili sauce, if desired. Serve hot.

****

Practical Variations

FRESH HO FUN SOUP

Substitute: ***1 pound fresh ho fun*** for the ***fresh Chinese noodles*** Cut ho fun
   into 1-inch wide strips. *Do not* parboil.

TIANJIN BEAN SHEET SOUP

Substitute: ***2 sheets Tianjin bean sheets*** for the ***fresh Chinese noodles*** Soak
   bean sheets in boiling water for 15 minutes to soften. Cut into about
   ½-inch wide strips. Immerse in cold water until ready to use. *Do not*
   parboil.

PORK WONTON SOUP

½ pound lean ground pork	) Combine
¼ cup coarsely chopped water chestnuts	) well in a
1 scallion Thinly sliced.	) bowl. This
3 - 5 dried Chinese mushrooms Soak at least ½ hour	) is the wonton
to soften. Squeeze out excess water, remove and dis-	) filling.
card stems. Finely chop caps (about 3 tablespoons)	) Can be done
½ teaspoon kosher salt or to taste	) a day ahead
2 teaspoons ginger wine, p. 16	) and refriger-
2 teaspoons regular soy sauce	) ated.

½ - ¾ pound ready-made wonton wrappers (about 45)
1 - 2 pounds bok choy Wash well. Slant-cut into about ½-inch thick slices.
1 small carrot Thinly sliced
6 - 8 cups broth

(1) Assemble wontons according to instructions on page 33. Place on a dry plate and cover with a dry towel.

(2) In a large pot, bring 3 quarts water to boil. Drop wontons into boiling water, stirring gently every now and then to prevent them from sticking together. Bring to boil. Reduce heat to medium, cook uncovered until wontons float to the top. Simmer 1 - 2 minutes or until wontons are cooked. Drain. Cool under cold running water. Drain well. May freeze at this point, see page 33.

(3) In a large pot, bring broth to boil. Add vegetables and desired amount of wontons. Bring to boil. Simmer until vegetables reach desired doneness and wontons are heated through. Serve hot.

KITCHEN HINT: Other vegetables may be added or substituted for bok choy.

****

Practical Variations

CHICKEN WONTON SOUP

Substitute: *½ pound ground chicken* for the *ground pork*

SEAFOOD WONTON SOUP

Substitute: *½ pound coarsely chopped shrimp* or *lobster* for *ground pork*
           ¼ cup coarsely chopped bamboo shoots for *water chestnuts*
Add: *1 - 2 tablespoons chopped Chinese parsley* to mixture.

WONTON SOUP (continued)

TO FREEZE WONTONS

Method 1: Place cooled and drained wontons single layer on plastic wrap lined baking pan, leaving a little space between each. Cover with plastic wrap and freeze. Once frozen, remove to a freezer bag or freezer container. Date and label. Return to freezer.

Method 2: Package cooled wontons into meal-size portions in freezer bag or freezer container. Date and label.

To serve: Thaw completely. Add to boiling broth.

How to assemble soup wontons

❶ Dip a finger in water and moisten three (3) edges of a wonton skin.

❷ Place about 1 teaspoon filling in middle of the unmoistened edge.

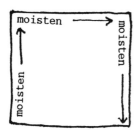

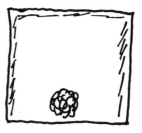

❸ Fold over edge with filling ⅓.

❹ Fold over another ⅓.

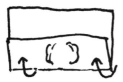

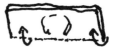

❺ With thumbs and forefingers holding the 2 ends, press to seal and at the same time pull down, overlapping the 2 lower corners. Press the corners together to seal. (If corners do not seal, moisten with a little water and press.)

Hot Pot (Chinese Fondue)

½ pound lean pork	) Slice against the
½ pound top sirloin or *flank steak*	) grain as thinly as
½ pound skinless and boneless chicken breast	) possible.

¾ - 1 pound raw shrimp Shelled (leave tail on.) Deveined. Butterfly, p. 35

1 pound squid Clean. Score. Cut into about 1½- x 1-inch pieces, p. 35

1 or more pounds napa cabbage Cut into 1- or 2-inch lengths

¼ - ½ pound snow peas Stringed and washed

½ - 1 pound fresh Chinese egg noodles Parboil 5 - 7 minutes. Cool under cold running water. Drained

8 - 16 ounces soft tofu Cut into about 1-inch cubes.

8 cups chicken broth

boiling water

Sauce for Hot Pot, p. 35

(1) Arrange meats, sea foods, vegetables, tofu and noodles attractively on serving platters, individually or combined.

(2) Place Chinese electric hot pot, electric wok or electric frying pan at center of table. Add broth. Bring to a boil and maintain boiling throughout the meal. Arrange platters of food around cooking appliance.

(3) Set out a soup bowl, a soup spoon, a fondue strainer and 2 pairs of chopsticks for each guest (one pair for cooking the other pair for eating.)

(4) Spoon 1 - 2 tablespoons sauce into each soup bowl. Place remaining sauce on dining table.

(5) Each guest will place 1 or more pieces of meat, seafood, tofu or vegetable in strainer. Place strainer in boiling broth. Cook food to desired doneness. Dip in sauce and enjoy. As broth level decreases due to evaporation, add boiling water to maintain level of liquid needed for cooking.

(6) Towards the end of the meal, place noodles in broth. Ladle hot noodles and some broth into bowl and enjoy.

****

Practical Variations

Seafood Hot Pot

Substitute: *Sea scallops, oysters* and *fish* for the *pork, beef* and *chicken*

Practical Variations(continued)

MONGOLIAN HOT POT

Substitute: ***2 pounds leg of lamb*** for the ***pork, beef, chicken*** and ***seafood***
6 - 8 ounces bean thread for the ***noodles*** Soak bean thread in
warm water at least 15 minutes to soften. Cut into shorter lengths.

SAUCE FOR HOT POT

1 tablespoon hoisin sauce	)
1 tablespoon tomato ketchup	) Combine all ingredients, or any
1 tablespoon Asian sesame seed	) combination, in a serving bowl.
paste or *peanut butter*	) This is the sauce.
1 tablespoon Asian sesame oil	)
3 tablespoons regular soy sauce	) Or place each ingredient in
¼ - 1 teaspoon Asian chili sauce	) separate dish and allow diner
1 clove garlic Pureed	) to create his/her own sauce
1 - 2 teaspoons finely minced	) combination.
white part of scallion	)

To butterfly shrimp:

❶ Remove shell, but leave the tail on. Devein. Rinse and pat dry.

❷ Place the shrimp flat on a cutting board.

❸ Cut along the back to split the shrimp lengthwise, but do not cut all the way
through.

❹ Flatten the shrimp.

To clean squid:

❶ Pull off the head and the tentacles. Cut off the tentacles just below the eyes.
Save the tentacles. Discard the rest.

❷ Peel off and discard the layer of purple membrane from the body.

❸ Slit open the squid. Remove and discard the cartilage and any jellylike
things inside. Rinse and dry well.

❹ Score the INSIDE surface by first cutting shallow parallel
lines about ¼-inch apart, over the whole body. Make
another set of parallel lines crisscrossing the
first set of parallel lines.

❺ Cut scored squid into desired size pieces.

TARO CONGEE

¹⁄₄ cup white glutinous rice) Washed and drained. *¹⁄₂ cup long* or *short grain white rice*)

2 - 3 quarts chicken broth

2 slices ginger

1 pound taro root Peeled. Cut into about ½-inch cubes. Pan-fry or deep-fry
    until lightly browned on all sides. Drain and reserve.

¹⁄₄ pound lean ground pork

¹⁄₂ pound frozen peas & carrots

1 - 2 scallions Thinly sliced.

(1) Place rice, broth and ginger in a sa bo (sandpot) for soup or large stockpot.
    Bring to boil, over medium heat. Lower heat. Simmer, covered, 3 - 4 hours.

(2) Stir in pork. Break up any lumps. Add taro. Bring to boil. Simmer 30 mins.

(3) Stir in peas & carrots. Simmer another 5 minutes. Stir in scallion. Serve hot.

SA BO FOR SOUP (CHINESE SANDPOT FOR SOUP)

SA BO (Chinese sandpot) is a traditional Chinese cooking pot made from fine
sand and clay. Sa bos come in different sizes and shapes and are used on top of
the range. Do not cook above medium high on the range. They also can be used
in the oven. If using in the oven, place it in a cold oven, not a preheated one,
with oven temperature no higher than 350°. To prevent cracking, do not place a
hot sa bo on a cold surface nor pour cold liquid into a hot sa bo.

New sa bo should be immersed completely in water for 24 - 48 hours, then wash
thoroughly with soap and water. Your sa bo is now ready to use. After each use,
wash in warm soapy water. Do not use abrasives.

Should your sa bo develop a crack or small leak, it is
still usable. Continue cooking in it, using low temperature, after 2 or more uses, it will heal itself.

The sa bo at right is for soup. The inside has a dark
brown glaze while the outside is unglazed for good
heat absorption. It is shaped like a beanpot to mini-
mize loss of moisture. The cover is unglazed and has
a hole in the center for ventilation and to prevent
boil-over. For all purpose sa bo see page 119.

RICE CONGEE WITH BEEF

serves 6 - 10

½ pound lean beef Cut across the grain into thin bite-sized pieces	)
	)
¼ teaspoon kosher salt or to taste	) Combine in a bowl.
2 teaspoons cornstarch	) Marinate 2 hours, if time
1 teaspoon regular soy sauce	) permits.
1 tablespoon oil	) Can be done the day before
1 tablespoon water	) and refrigerated.
2 slices ginger	)

¼ cup white glutinous rice	) Washed and drained.
½ cup long or **short grain white rice**	)

2 - 3 quarts chicken broth

1 scallion Thinly sliced	)
2 - 4 tablespoons ja choy	) These are served as condiments.
(*Szechuan preserved vegetables*)	) Place each in a separate little
Asian sesame oil	) dish at the center of the table.
Asian chili oil or **chili sauce**	) Serve all or any combination.
Chinese parsley Coarsely chopped	)

(1) Place rice and broth in a sa bo (sandpot) for soup, p. 36, or large stockpot. Bring to boil, over medium heat. Lower heat and simmer, covered, 3 - 4 hours. (Up to this point can be done the day before and reheat using low temperature.)

(2) Stir in beef. Bring to a boil. Ladle into individual bowls. Serve hot. Diner adds own condiments.

KITCHEN HINT: For a nuttier flavor and different texture substitute brown glutinous rice for the white glutinous rice and substitute brown long or brown short grain rice for the white rice.

****

Practical Variations

CHICKEN CONGEE

Substitute: *½ pound boneless* and *skinless chicken breast* for the **beef**

FISH CONGEE

Substitute: *½ - ¾ pound mild flavored fish fillet* for the **beef**

PORK CONGEE

2 pounds pork bones	) Combine. Marinate overnight, or up to 2
1 tablespoon kosher salt	) days, in refrigerator.

2 - 3 preserved eggs

½ cup long or **short grain white rice**

¼ cup shelled raw peanuts Cover with boiling water. Let stand about 30
    minutes. Remove brown outer skin.

2 slices fresh ginger

2 - 3 quarts cold water

1 scallion Thinly sliced	) These are served as condiments.
Asian sesame oil	) Place each in a separate little
Asian chili oil or **Asian chili sauce**	) dish at the center of the table.
Chinese parsley Coarsely chopped.	) Serve all or any combination.

(1) Place rice, peanuts, ginger and water in a sa bo (sandpot) for soup, p. 36, or
    4-quart stockpot.

(2) Rinse marinated pork bones and add to pot.

(3) Shell preserved eggs. Rinse. Cut into quarters and add to pot.

(4) Bring to boil, over medium heat. Lower heat and simmer, covered, 3 - 4
    hours. (Up to this point can be done the day before and reheat using low
    temperature.)

(5) Ladle congee into individual soup bowls. Serve hot. Each diner adds
    condiments to taste.

KITCHEN HINT: For a different flavor and a different texture, substitute brown glutinous rice for
        the peanuts.

****

Practical Variation

PORK CHICKEN AND LETTUCE CONGEE

Add: **½ - 1 cooked chicken breast** Finely shred along the grain, using
    fingers.

    ½ - 1 head iceberg lettuce Finely shredded.

    Add chicken and lettuce at the end of step (4) above. Bring to a boil. Serve
    hot.

SHRIMP & BEAN THREADS SOUP serves 3 - 4

4 ounces raw shrimp Shelled.)	
Deveined. Split in half)	Combine.
lengthwise or leave whole)	Can be done the day before and
¼ teaspoon kosher salt)	refrigerated.
2 slices fresh ginger)	

2 ounces lean pork Shredded)	Combine.
1 teaspoon regular soy sauce)	Can be done the day before and
dash of white pepper or to taste)	refrigerated.

1 tablespoon cloud ears Soak in water at least ½ hour to soften. Remove and discard any sandy and woody parts.

30 tiger lily flowers Soak in water at least ½ hour to soften. Remove and discard any woody parts. Tie into a knot (optional).

2 ounces bean threads Soak in water 15 minutes. Cut into 2-inch lengths.

4 - 5 cups chicken broth

1 scallion Thinly sliced.

Asian chili oil or **Asian chili sauce** (optional)

(1) Bring broth to boil. Add shrimp and pork. Bring to boil.

(2) Add cloud ears, tiger lily flowers and bean threads. Bring to boil. Simmer 3 minutes. Stir in scallion and chili, if using. Serve hot.

KITCHEN HINT: Bean threads can absorb a great deal of liquid. Soup will thicken if allowed to stand after bean threads are added.

****

Practical Variations

CHICKEN, TOFU & BEAN THREAD SOUP

Substitute: **4 ounces boneless** and **skinless chicken breast** for the **shrimp**
Slice chicken into thin bite-size slices.

4 ounces soft or **firm tofu** for the **pork** Cut tofu into bite-size cubes or slices.

SPICY NOODLES SOUP

serves 3 - 4

8 ounces lean pork Shredded	)
½ teaspoon kosher salt or to taste	) Combine and marinate.
2 teaspoons ginger wine, p. 16	) Can be done the day before
2 slices ginger from ginger wine	) and refrigerated.
2 teaspoons regular soy sauce	)
dash white pepper or to taste	)

½ cup shredded bamboo shoots

¼ - ½ cup shredded ja choy (*Szechuan preserved vegetables*)

3 - 5 dried Chinese mushrooms Soak in water at least ½ hour to soften. Squeeze out excess water. Remove and discard stems. Shred caps.

8 ounces creamy-Chinese style dried noodles Parboil 7 minutes. Drained. Cool under cold running water. Drained. Set aside.

1 - 2 scallion Cleaned. Shredded or sliced thinly.

6 cups chicken broth

2 - 3 tablespoons oil

1 teaspoon cornstarch	) Combine in a small bowl.
1 tablespoon water	) Stir well just before adding to wok.

(1) Heat wok. Add oil. Swirl to coat wok. Add pork. Stir-fry over high heat until color changes. Add bamboo shoots, ja choy and mushrooms. Mix well. Add ¼ cup broth. Bring to a boil. Cover. Simmer 3 minutes. Thicken with cornstarch mixture. Remove to a bowl. (This step can be done the day before, cooled and refrigerated. Reheat before serving.)

(2) Bring remaining broth to boil. Add noodles. Bring to boil. Simmer until noodles are heated through or reach desired doneness.

(3) Spoon noodles and broth into individual soup bowls. Top with a portion of pork mixture. Sprinkle scallion on top. Serve hot.

KITCHEN HINT: Substitute Shanghai dried noodles, u-don noodles, buckwheat noodles or linguine for creamy-Chinese style dried noodles.

40 Soup   My Students' Favorite Chinese Recipes, updated edition

VELVET CHICKEN & SWEET CORN CHOWDER

serves 4 - 6

4 - 6 ounces finely minced chicken breast	) Combine chicken,
2 egg whites Lightly beaten	) egg whites, salt and
½ teaspoon kosher salt or to taste	) pepper. Gradually
dash of white pepper or to taste	) blend in chicken
½ cup room temperature chicken broth	) broth. Set aside.

1 15-ounce can cream-style corn
4 - 6 cups chicken broth
1 - 2 egg yolks Lightly beaten and scrambled. Chop finely or cut into thin
    strips.
Chinese parsley or *regular parsley for garnish*
¼ teaspoon Asian sesame oil or to taste (optional)

(1) In a large pot, bring broth to boil. Add sweet corn and stir. While stirring, slowly add chicken mixture, stirring all the time to prevent chicken mixture from lumping.
(2) Bring to boil, using medium to medium-high heat. Stir in sesame oil.
(3) Ladle into individual bowls. Garnish with parsley and egg yolks. Serve hot.

KITCHEN HINT: Cut chicken breast into chunks. Add to bowl of food processor together with egg whites, salt, pepper and broth. Pulse a few seconds to desired texture.

KITCHEN HINT: For a thicker soup, use the lesser quantity of broth. For a thinner soup use the larger quantity of broth.

****

Practical Variations

VELVET CHICKEN, TOFU & SWEET CORN CHOWDER

Use: *2 ounces finely minced chicken breast* and *4 ounces soft* or *firm tofu* Mash tofu with a fork.

Substitute: *Thinly sliced green part of scallion* for the *parsley*

VELVET SCALLOPS & SWEET CORN CHOWDER

Substitute: *4 - 6 ounces sea scallops* for the *chicken breast*
Add: *¼ teaspoon Chinese red vinegar* to individual bowl of soup.

WATERCRESS SOUP

serves 5 - 7

½ pound lean beef Cut across the grain into thin bite-size slices	)
2 teaspoons cornstarch	) Combine.
1½ teaspoons regular soy sauce	) Marinate 2 hours if time
1 tablespoon oil	) permits.
1 tablespoon water	) Can be done the day
2 slices ginger	) before and refrigerated.
	)

2 bunches watercress Wash well in 2 - 3 changes of water. Discard any yellowing parts and tough stems. Drained. Leave whole or cut into smaller sections. Use both leaves and stems.

6 - 8 cups chicken broth

1 - 2 scallions, white part only Shredded or thinly sliced.

½ teaspoon Asian sesame oil or to taste

(1) In large pot, bring broth to boil. Add watercress. Bring to a boil. Simmer to desired doneness. (For crunchy watercress, simmer for 2 minutes. For softer texture and a stronger flavored soup, simmer 1 - 2 hours.)

(2) Stir in beef. Bring to boil. Stir in sesame oil. Ladle into individual soup bowls. Sprinkle scallion on top and serve hot.

****

Practical Variations

SPINACH TOFU SOUP

Substitute: *1 pound spinach* for the *watercress*. Wash spinach well. Use both leaves and stems. Blanch in boiling water for 10 seconds. Drain and cool under cold running water. Drain again and squeeze out excess water. Cut into shorter lengths or chop coarsely. Simmer 2 minutes.

Add: *4 - 8 ounces soft* or *firm tofu* Cut tofu into bite-sized pieces. Add at the same time as beef.

BROCCOLI RABE SOUP

Substitute: *½ - ¾ pound broccoli rabe* for the *watercress* Blanch in boiling water for 5 seconds. Drain and cool under cold running water. Drain again and squeeze out excess water. Cut into shorter lengths. Simmer 2 - 4 minutes.

WINTERMELON SOUP

serves 4 - 6

1 - 2 pounds wintermelon Peeled. Remove and discard seeds. Cut into about ½-inch cubes

2 ounces pork or *chicken*	)
2 ounces ham	)
2 ounces shelled and deveined raw shrimp	) Cut all to about the
4 Chinese dried mushrooms Soak in water	) size of green peas.
at least ½ hour to soften. Squeeze out	)
excess water. Remove and discard stems.	)

1 - 2 tablespoons green peas
1 scallion Thinly sliced
4 cups chicken broth
¼ teaspoon Asian sesame oil or to taste

(1) In large pot, bring broth to boil. Add wintermelon. Boil about 3 minutes.
(2) Add pork and mushrooms. Bring to a boil. Add ham, shrimp and green peas. Bring to a boil. Simmer 1 - 2 minutes or until pork is cooked. Stir in scallion and sesame oil. Serve hot.

****

Practical Variations

CUCUMBER SOUP
Substitute: *2 cucumbers* for the *wintermelon* Peel cucumber. Cut in half lengthwise. Remove and discard seeds. Cut into ½-inch cubes.

ZUCCHINI SOUP
Substitute: *1 pound zucchini* for the *wintermelon* Cut zucchini in half lengthwise. Remove and discard seeds. Cut into ½-inch cubes.

CHAYOTE SOUP
Substitute: *2 - 3 chayote* for the *wintermelon* Peel chayote. Cut in half lengthwise. Remove and discard seed. Cut into ½-inch cubes.

BOILED MEATBALL SOUP

½ pound ground meat (pork, beef, veal, turkey or *chicken)*	) Combine. Mix well in one
2 tablespoons cornstarch	) direction until somewhat
1 tablespoon minced scallion	) elastic. Can be done ahead
1 egg white or *½ of a beaten egg*	) of time and refrigerated.
¼ teaspoon kosher salt or to taste	) *This is the meat mixture.*
¼ teaspoon grated ginger	) Make into about ½-inch
2 teaspoons regular soy sauce	) meatballs.
	)

4 - 8 ounces rice sticks Soak in lukewarm water for 5 minutes. Drain well before adding to broth.

vegetables of choice Cut into bite-sized pieces.

6 - 8 cups chicken broth

shredded or thinly sliced scallion for garnish

Chinese parsley for garnish

¼ - ½ teaspoon Asian sesame oil or to taste

¼ - ½ teaspoon Asian chili sauce or *chili oil or to taste*

(1) In a large pot, bring broth to boil, using medium heat.

(2) Drop meatballs into boiling broth. Return to a boil. Cook, uncovered, until meatballs float to the surface.

(3) Add vegetables. Bring to a boil. Cook, uncovered, until vegetables are slightly under desired doneness.

(4) Add drained ricesticks. Bring to a boil. Cook another 2 - 3 minutes or until rice sticks are tender. Stir in sesame oil and chili, if using. Garnish with scallion and Chinese parsley.

VEGETABLES SUGGESTION: bok choy, napa, broccoli, cabbage, carrots, choy sum, broccoli rabe, zucchini, mushrooms, snowpeas, bean sprouts, angled luffa, lettuce and spinach.

NOTE: Precooked noodles or pasta can be substituted for the rice sticks.
****

Practical Variation

MEATCAKE SOUP

❶ Spread meat mixture into a preheated and oiled 10" or 12" frying pan. (DO NOT make meatballs.) Cook until golden brown. Cut into ¼'s. Turn and brown the other side, adding more oil as needed.

❷ Remove cooked meatcake and cut into bite-sized pieces.

❸ Skip step (2) above. Continue with steps (3) and (4) above.

RICE

ALL ABOUT RICE

BROWN RICE: Available as long grain, medium grain and short grain. All are interchangeable in cooking. Cooked long grain brown rice has a firm, dry texture. Cooked medium and short grain brown rice has a softer texture than long grain brown rice. All have a nice nutty flavor. Since only the outer husk, but not the bran and rice germ, is removed from brown rice, it has a higher fiber content and is richer in nutrients.

WHITE RICE: Available as long grain, medium grain and short grain. Cooked long grain white rice has a firm, dry texture and the cooked rice separates easily. Cooked medium and short grain white rice has a softer texture and tends to be sticky. White rice is brown rice that went through further processing to remove the brown layer of bran and the rice germ, leaving only the white starchy kernel. Because all of the nutrients were removed during the processing, white rice as we know it, has been enriched by coating the kernels with a solution of the nutrients lost during processing.

SCENTED RICE: During cooking, scented rice gives off a popcorn-like aroma. The most aromatic of the scented rice is basmati rice, also known as Indian rice. Another widely available scented rice is jasmine rice also known as Thai rice or Chinese rice. These rice are available in both brown and white form.

GLUTINOUS RICE: Available as long grain, medium grain and short grain and in brown, black or white form. White glutinous rice is white in the raw state, but becomes opaque after cooking. Also known as sweet rice and sticky rice (the cooked rice is very sticky). Because white glutinous rice burns easily the preferred cooking method is steaming. Brown or black glutinous, however, can be cooked on the range. Glutinous rice is not used as a substitute for regular rice.

BLACK AND RED LONG GRAIN RICE: These rice with their bran and rice germ intact, when cooked, have a dry texture and earthy, nutty flavor.

CONVERTED RICE: Converted rice is white or brown rice that went through a steaming process during milling, forcing some of the nutrients to penetrate into the center of the grain. Converted rice is also known as parboiled rice.

MINUTE RICE: Minute rice cooks very fast. It is white or brown rice that has been precooked and dried requiring little time to reheat and serve. Minute rice is also known as instant or precooked rice.

PERFECT WHITE RICE

makes 6 cups

2 cups long or short grain white rice

(1) Place rice in a 2- or 3-quart pot. Rinse until water runs clear.

(2) With index finger touching the SURFACE of the rice, add cold water to reach the first joint of the first finger (about ⅞").

(3) Cook uncovered, using high heat, until most of the water has been absorbed and little craters begin to form on the surface of the rice. (*Do not* stir and *do not* lower the heat during this cooking period.) At this point, reduce heat to a simmer.

(4) Cover pot and simmer rice for 15 minutes. DO NOT peek during this simmering period. At the end of 15 minutes, fluff rice and serve. If not serving at once, cover pot after fluffing and leave on warm range until ready to use.

NOTE: Fingertip should touch the SURFACE of the rice not through to the bottom of the pot. If using the above method and your rice comes out too dry or undercooked, it means the first joint of your finger is shorter than mine. Increase the amount of water and make a note on the recipe. If your rice comes out too soft and sticky, it means the first joint of your finger is longer than mine. Decrease the amount of water, and again, make a note on the recipe.

NOTE: The above method for cooking white rice and the method for cooking brown rice on page 48, will work for any quantity of rice. The reason is, when cooking a larger quantity (more than 2 cups) of rice we automatically reach for a larger pot and when cooking a smaller quantity (less than 2 cups) of rice we automatically reach for a smaller pot ensuring that the ratio of water to rice is correct.

KITCHEN HINT: When cooking rice, do not stir. Stirring breaks the coating of the rice releasing starch that sinks and sticks to the bottom of the pot causing the rice to burn. This is also true when boiling peeled or sliced potatoes. There is less chance of potatoes burning if you refrain from stirring.

KITCHEN HINT: Reheat leftover rice, white or brown, in the microwave or by steaming.

KITCHEN HINT: When cooking rice, white or brown, make extra for fried rice.

KITCHEN HINT: To clean pot that has rice sticking to the bottom, add cold water to pot, soak for about 10 minutes. Clean. This works well for any starchy food.

BOILED BROWN RICE

makes 6 cups

2 cups long, medium or short grain brown rice

(1) Place rice in a 2 or 3-quart pot. Rinse to get rid of any chaff and husks.

(2) With index finger touching the SURFACE of the rice, add cold water to reach ⅛-inch above the first joint of the first finger (about 1").

(3) Cook uncovered, using high heat, until little craters begin to form on the surface of the rice and there is still a thin layer of water covering the surface. (*Do not* stir and *do not* lower the heat during this cooking period.) At this point, reduce heat to a simmer.

(4) Cover pot and simmer rice for 20 minutes. DO NOT peek during this simmering period. At the end of 20 minutes, fluff rice and serve. If not serving at once, cover pot after fluffing and leave on warm range until ready to use.

NOTE: Read NOTES and KITCHEN HINTS on page 47.

KITCHEN HINT: Cooked brown rice freezes well. Make extra for the freezer.

****

Practical Variation

BROWN RICE WITH ADZUKI BEAN

Add: *1 - 1½ cups parboiled adzuki beans* Add during step (2) after correct amount of water is added to rice.

To parboil adzuki beans: ❶ Rinse adzuki beans. Discard any that floats.

❷ Add to pot and cover with about 3 inches of cold water or 3 to 4 times as much water as beans. Bring to boil. Cover and simmer 3 minutes.

❸ Let stand, covered, 1 - 2 hours.

❹ Drain.

NOTE: The black bean paste in black bean cakes, mooncakes and other pastries are made with pureed adzuki beans.

KITCHEN HINT: Parboiled adzuki beans freeze well. Make extra for the freezer. Package in appropriate amounts, date, label and freeze. Can be used frozen or thawed.

HAM & EGGS FRIED RICE

serves 3 - 5

4 cups boiled white rice Fluffed and cooled.
2 eggs Lightly beaten
4 ounces cooked ham Diced
¾ cup frozen peas & carrots Thawed
1 scallion Thinly sliced.
1 teaspoon kosher salt or to taste
1 tablespoon regular soy sauce
3 tablespoons oil
white or *black pepper to taste*
1 - 2 teaspoons sesame oil (optional)

(1) Heat wok. Add 1 tablespoon oil. Swirl to coat wok. Add eggs. Scramble over high heat until just set. Remove to a plate and cut into small pieces.
(2) Add 1 tablespoon oil to wok. Add peas & carrots. Stir-fry 1 minute. Add ham. Stir-fry another minute. Remove to a plate and set aside.
(3) Add 1 tablespoon oil to wok. Add salt and rice. Stir-fry until rice is coated with oil and heated through. Mix in soy sauce.
(4) Add ham, peas & carrots and scallion. Mix well. Stir in scrambled eggs, white or black pepper and sesame oil. Serve hot.

NOTE: Any kind of precooked meat can be used as substitute for the ham. This is a great recipe for some the precooked (please do not say leftover) Thanksgiving turkey.
KITCHEN HINT: To give a darker color to the rice, substitute dark or mushroom soy sauce for the regular soy sauce.

****

Practical Variations

PINEAPPLE HAM FRIED RICE

Add: *1 - 2 tablespoons dark* or *mushroom soy sauce* at the end of step (3) and reduce or eliminate the *salt*
½ cup (or more) pineapple tidbits during step (4)

MIXED VEGETABLES FRIED RICE

Substitute: *¾ cup frozen mixed vegetables,* thawed, for the *peas & carrots*

NUTS FRIED RICE

Substitute: *4 ounces roasted, unsalted nuts,* coarsely chopped, for the *ham*

My Students' Favorite Chinese Recipes, updated edition

Rice **49**

BEEF FRIED RICE

4 cups boiled white rice Fluffed and cooled.

2 eggs Lightly beaten

6 - 8 ounces lean ground beef

½ cup frozen peas & carrots Thawed

¼ - ½ cup frozen corn Thawed

¼ - ½ cup diced or thinly sliced celery

¼ cup diced onion

1 clove garlic Minced

1 scallion Thinly sliced.

1 tablespoon ginger wine, p. 16

1 - 2 tablespoons dark or *mushroom soy sauce*

½ teaspoon kosher salt or to taste

¼ teaspoon ground black or *white pepper or to taste*

3 tablespoons oil

1 - 2 teaspoons sesame oil (optional)

(1) Heat wok. Add 1 tablespoon oil. Swirl to coat wok. Add eggs. Scramble over high heat until just set. Remove to a plate and cut into small pieces.

(2) Add 1 tablespoon oil to wok. Add peas & carrots, corn and celery. Stir-fry 2 minutes or until heated through. Remove to a plate and set aside.

(3) Add 1 tablespoon oil to wok. Add onion and garlic. Stir-fry until onion is translucent. Add beef. Stir-fry until beef is lightly browned. Add ginger wine, 1 tablespoon soy sauce and ground pepper. Mix well.

(4) Add salt and rice. Stir-fry until rice is heated through. Add more soy sauce, 1 teaspoon at a time, until desired color is reached.

(5) Add vegetables, scallion, eggs and sesame oil. Mix well. Serve hot.

Practical Variation

TURKEY FRIED RICE WITH BEAN SPROUTS

Substitute: *6 - 8 ounces ground turkey* for the *ground beef*

8 ounces bean sprouts for the *peas & carrots, corn* and *celery*
Stir-fry bean sprouts during step (2) for 2 - 3 minutes or until they lose their raw taste.

CURRIED SHRIMP FRIED RICE

serves 3 - 5

4 cups boiled white rice Fluffed and cooled.

2 eggs Lightly beaten

6 - 8 ounces shelled and deveined shrimp Diced

1 cup bite-sized pieces broccoli florets

½ cup diced red pepper

½ cup diced or sliced mushrooms

¼ cup diced onion

1 clove garlic Minced

1 scallion Thinly sliced.

1 tablespoon ginger wine p. 16

1 - 2 tablespoons regular soy sauce

½ teaspoon kosher salt or to taste

¼ teaspoon ground black or *white pepper or to taste*

1 - 3 teaspoons curry powder or to taste

4 tablespoons oil

2 - 3 tablespoons broth or *water* *(or as needed)*

1 - 2 teaspoons sesame oil *(optional)*

(1) Heat wok. Add 1 tablespoon oil. Swirl to coat wok. Add eggs. Scramble over high heat until just set. Remove to a plate and cut into small pieces.

(2) Add 1 tablespoon oil to wok. Add broccoli, red pepper and mushroom. Stir-fry over high heat until broccoli changes color. Remove to a plate.

(3) Add 2 tablespoons oil to wok. Add onion and garlic. Stir-fry over medium heat until onion is translucent. Add shrimp, ginger wine, ground pepper and curry. Stir-fry until shrimp changes color, adding broth or water 1 tablespoon at a time if wok is dry.

(4) Add salt and rice. Stir-fry until rice is heated through, adding broth or water 1 tablespoon at a time if wok is dry. Add soy sauce to taste.

(5) Add vegetables, scallion, eggs and sesame oil. Mix well. Serve hot.

****

Practical Variation

CURRIED PORK FRIED RICE

Substitute: *6 - 8 ounces coarse ground pork* for the *shrimp*

STEAMED GLUTINOUS RICE

serves 3 - 5

1 cup white glutinous rice Wash and drain well in a strainer. Place in a large bowl. Add *1½ cups chicken broth*. Soak for at least 2 hours in the refrigerator.

3 - 4 dried Chinese mushrooms Soak in water at least ½ hour to soften. Squeeze out excess water. Remove and discard stems. Dice caps.

2 ounces ham Diced

1 Chinese sausage Diced or thinly sliced

¼ cup diced bamboo shoots

½ cup frozen peas & carrots Thawed

2 teaspoons dark or *mushroom soy sauce*

dash of white pepper or to taste

1 tablespoon oil

1 scallion Cleaned. Sliced thinly, green and white parts.

(1) Heat wok. Add oil. Swirl to coat wok. Add sausage. Stir-fry over medium heat until some of the fat is rendered. Add mushrooms, ham and bamboo shoots. Stir-fry 1 minute.

(2) Add rice, broth, soy sauce and pepper. Stir-fry over medium-high heat until broth has been absorbed.

(3) Transfer rice mixture to a heatproof dish. Steam on high for 30 minutes. (Up to this point can be done ahead of time. Cool and refrigerate up to a day or freeze for longer storage. Steam to reheat.)

(4) Stir-in peas & carrots. Steam 2 more minutes. Sprinkle scallion on top. Serve hot.

Practical Variation

STEAMED GLUTINOUS RICE WITH GINGKO NUTS

Add: *½ - ¾ cup shelled fresh gingko nuts* Place gingko nuts in a container. Cover with boiling water. Let stand 30 minutes. Remove and discard brown skin. Add gingko nuts during step (2).

STEAMED GLUTINOUS RICE WITH PANCETTA

Substitute: *4 ounces diced pancetta* for the *ham* and *Chinese sausage*

NOODLES & DOUGH

CHA-SHAO CHOW MEIN

serves 3 - 5

¾ - 1 pound fresh mein (Chinese noodles) Parboil 6 minutes. Drain. Cool
under cold running water. Drain again.

6 - 8 ounces cha-shao (Chinese roast pork)

1 pound mung bean sprouts Washed. Discard soft discolored sprouts and
bean shells that float to the top. Drained

1 carrot Peeled and shredded

4 - 6 dried Chinese mushrooms Soak in water at least ½ hour to soften.
Squeeze out excess water. Remove and discard stems. Shred caps.

1 scallion Shredded or thinly sliced.

2 slices ginger from ginger wine, p. 16

1 teaspoon kosher salt or to taste

4 tablespoons oil

½ cup chicken or *pork broth*	)
1 tablespoon ginger wine, p. 16	) Combine in a small bowl.
1 tablespoon oyster sauce	) This is the sauce.
1 tablespoon regular soy sauce	)
dash of white/black pepper or to taste	)

2 teaspoons cornstarch	) Combine in a small bowl.
2 tablespoons broth or water	) Stir well just before adding to wok.

(1) Heat wok. Add 2 tablespoons oil. Swirl to coat wok. Heat to near smoking.
Add noodles and stir-fry over medium-high to high heat until noodles are
heated through and evenly coated with oil. Spread on a large preheated
serving platter.

(2) Add 1 tablespoon oil to wok. Add ginger and mushrooms. Stir-fry over
medium heat about 1 minute or until mushrooms are fragrant. Add salt,
bean sprouts and carrots. Stir-fry over high heat until bean sprouts reach
desired doneness. Remove and discard ginger. Drain vegetables, reserving
the liquid, and arrange on top of noodles.

(3) Add 1 tablespoon oil to wok. Add roast pork. Stir-fry 1 minute. Add sauce
and reserved liquid from drained vegetables. Bring to boil. Thicken with
cornstarch mixture. Spoon over vegetables and noodles.

(4) Sprinkle scallion on top. Serve.

KITCHEN HINT: Short on time? Slice, not shred, the roast pork and carrot.

Practical Variations

PORTABELLA ROAST BEEF CHOW MEIN

Substitute: ***6 - 8 ounces roast beef*** for the ***cha shao*** Shred or slice roast beef.
1 pound portabella mushrooms for the ***bean sprouts***
Cut portabella into about ¼-inch thick slices.

ROAST TURKEY CHOW MEIN
(Another great way to enjoy the precooked [please do not say leftover] Thanksgiving turkey)

Substitute: ***6 - 8 ounces roast turkey*** for the ***cha shao*** Shred or slice turkey.
1 pound mixed vegetables for the ***bean sprouts***
Cut vegetables into bite-sized pieces.
Vegetables suggestion: broccoli, cauliflower, snow peas, celery, bok choy, kohlrabi, green beans, cabbage, zucchini, peppers, etc.

SHRIMP CHOW MEIN

Substitute: ***½ - ¾ pound raw shrimp*** for the ***cha shao*** Shell and devein shrimp. Toss with ¼ teaspoon of salt. During step (3) stir-fry until shrimp is cooked.

CHICKEN CHOW MEIN

Substitute: ***8 - 12 ounces chicken meat*** for the ***cha shao***
Marinate chicken with: ***1 tablespoon ginger wine***, p. 16
1 teaspoon dark soy sauce
1 teaspoon regular soy sauce
1 teaspoon sugar
½ teaspoon kosher salt or to taste
¼ - 1 teaspoon Asian chili sauce or to taste
During step (3) stir-fry until chicken is cooked.

KITCHEN HINT: 8 - 12 ounces of any pasta can be used as a substitute for the mein (Chinese noodles). Cook according to package directions.

EGG NOODLES WITH MEAT SAUCE

serves 3 - 4

1 pound lean ground pork
2 tablespoons oil
4 - 5 cloves garlic Minced
½ - 1 bunch scallion Thinly sliced
2 tablespoons ginger wine, p. 16
1 tablespoon dark or *mushroom soy sauce*
3 tablespoons Chinese bean sauce
½ teaspoon brown or *white sugar*
¾ - 1 cup chicken broth
1 - 2 large cucumbers Peeled. Cut in half, lengthwise. Remove and discard
  seeds. Shred or slice thinly. Place on a serving plate or serving bowl.
1 pound fresh Chinese egg noodles
2 teaspoons sesame oil

(1) Heat wok. Add 2 tablespoons oil. Swirl to coat wok. Add garlic and scallion.
    Stir-fry over medium-high heat for about 30 seconds. Add ground pork. Stir-
    fry over high heat until color changes. Add ginger wine and soy sauce. Stir-
    fry until wine and soy sauce are absorbed. Stir in bean sauce and sugar.
(2) Transfer meat to a saucepan. Add broth. Bring to a boil. Cover. Simmer until
    most of the broth has been absorbed, about 10 - 15 minutes. Transfer to a
    serving bowl. Can be made ahead of time.
(3) While meat sauce is simmering, bring a large pot of water to a boil. Add
    noodles. Cook, uncovered, over medium-high heat for 6 minutes. Drain.
    Arrange on a preheated serving platter or large bowl. Toss with sesame oil.
(4) To serve, place a portion of noodle on plate, top with some cucumber and
    meat sauce.

KITCHEN HINT: Meat sauce freezes well. Make extra for the freezer.
****

Practical Variation

SPAGHETTI WITH MEAT SAUCE

Substitute: *8 - 12 ounces No. 8 spaghetti* for the *Chinese noodles*

PERFECT NO. 8 SPAGHETTI

Bring a large pot of water to boil. Add spaghetti. Stir to loosen strands. Bring to
boil. Cover pot. Remove from heat. Let stand for 15 minutes, covered (do not
peek). Drain and serve.

OYSTER SAUCE NOODLES

1 pound fresh Chinese egg noodles
1 - 1½ cups about 1-inch lengths Chinese chives
    or ½ - 1 bunch scallion Shredded or thinly sliced
2 - 3 tablespoons oyster sauce
¼ teaspoon white pepper or to taste
1 - 2 tablespoons oil
1 - 2 teaspoons sesame oil (optional)
½ teaspoon kosher salt or to taste

(1) Cook noodles, uncovered, in large pot of boiling water until al dente, about 5 - 7 minutes. Drain well.

(2) While noodles are cooking, heat wok. Add oil. Swirl to coat wok. Add chives or scallion. Stir fry 30 seconds over medium-high heat. Add drained noodles. Toss well.

(3) Add oyster sauce, white pepper and sesame oil. Mix well. Add salt to taste. Serve hot or at room temperature.

KITCHEN HINT: For added texture and nutrients, toss in 2 or more tablespoons toasted sesame seeds, pine nuts or other toasted seeds or nuts.

****

Practical Variations

OYSTER SAUCE ROTINI

Substitute: *6 - 8 ounces packaged rotini* for the *egg noodles* Cook rotini 8 - 10 minutes or according to package directions.

Add: *¼ cup each coarsely chopped* or *shredded red* and *yellow peppers* during step (3).

OYSTER SAUCE FUSILLI

Substitute: *8 ounces packaged fusilli* for the *egg noodles*. Cook fusilli 15 minutes or according to package directions.

Add: *1 carrot* Shredded, during step (3).
    1 cup broccoli florets Cut to bite-sized and blanched 10 seconds, during step (3).

HONG KONG STYLE PAN FRIED NOODLES

serves 4 - 6

¾ - 1 pound Hong Kong style pan fried noodles Place noodles in a large pot of boiling water. Stir and drain. Cool under cold running water. Drain. Divide into 4 - 6 portions. Form each into a ½-inch thick noodle-pancake.

½ pound raw shrimp Shelled. Deveined.

¼ pound cooked meat (pork, ham, chicken or turkey) Thinly sliced.

1 can baby corn

1 carrot Peeled. Slant cut thinly.

¼ pound snow peas Stringed

1 small onion Cut into small chunks

2 slices ginger from ginger wine, p. 16

1 clove garlic Finely minced.

1 teaspoon kosher salt or to taste

½ cup oil (about)

1½ - 2 cups chicken broth	)
2 tablespoons ginger wine, p. 16	) Combine in a small bowl.
2 tablespoons oyster sauce	) This is the sauce.
1 teaspoon sugar	)
¼ teaspoon white pepper or to taste	)

2 tablespoons cornstarch)	Combine in a small dish.
3 tablespoons water)	Stir well just before adding to wok.

(1) Heat a large frying pan. Add 3 - 4 tablespoons oil. Heat to near smoking. Pan fry noodle-pancakes until golden brown on both sides, adding more oil as needed. Remove to preheated serving platter. (The outside of the noodle-pancake should be crisp while the inside remains soft.)

(2) Add 1 - 2 tablespoons oil to preheated wok. Add ginger and garlic. Stir-fry over medium-high heat for about 30 seconds. Add shrimp. Stir-fry over high heat until shrimp changes color. Add sliced meat. Stir-fry another 1 - 2 minutes. Remove to a plate. Remove and discard ginger.

(3) Add 1 tablespoon oil to wok, if needed. Add salt and vegetables. Stir-fry over high heat for about 2 minutes. Add sauce. Bring to a boil.

(4) Stir in shrimp and meat. Bring to a boil. Thicken with cornstarch mixture.

(5) Spoon over noodle-pancakes. Serve at once.

BROILED HONG KONG STYLE PAN FRIED NOODLES

❶ Skip step (1) on page 58.

❷ Place noodle-pancakes on a generously oiled rimmed baking sheet or shallow baking pan, leaving a little space between each.

❸ Brush noodle-pancakes with oil.

❹ Broil, in middle of oven, for 5 minutes, or until golden and crisp.

❺ Turn noodle-pancakes, broil another 5 minutes, or until golden and crisp. Remove to a preheated serving platter.

❻ Continue with steps (2), (3), (4) and (5) on page 58.

STIR-FRIED HONG KONG STYLE PAN FRIED NOODLES

❶ Cut cooled and drained parboiled noodles into shorter lengths, if desired. Do not divide and do not make into noodle-pancakes.

❷ Skip step (1) on page 58.

❸ Heat wok. Add 2 tablespoons oil. Add noodles. Stir-fry until noodles are heated through. Remove and arrange on a preheated serving platter.

❹ Continue with steps (2), (3) and (4) on page 58.

❺ Skip step (5) on page 58.

❻ Spoon mixture over stir-fried noodles and serve.

STIR-FRIED HONG KONG STYLE PAN FRIED NOODLES 2

❶ While water to parboil noodles is heating go to cooking instructions.

❷ Skip step (1) on page 58.

❸ Continue with steps (2), (3) and (4) on page 58.

❹ Cut noodles into shorter lengths, if desired. Place in boiling water. Stir and drain. Add to wok. Mix well and serve.

❺ Skip step (5) on page 58.

NOTE: Hong Kong style pan fried noodles are thin Chinese egg noodles that have been pre-cooked by steaming. If unavailable, substitute fresh or dried thin Chinese egg noodles, cooked al dente, cooled and drained. Thin spaghetti or vermicelli also make good substitute.

BEEF HO FUN

serves 3 - 6

1½ - 2 pounds fresh ho fun (rice noodles) Cut into about ½-inch wide strips. Drop into boiling water, stir to separate strips. Drained.

½ pound flank or *top sirloin steak* Cut across the grain into thin bite-sized pieces.	) Combine.
1 teaspoon cornstarch	) Marinate, if time
½ teaspoon sugar	) permits. Can be done
1 tablespoon ginger wine, p. 16	) the day before and
1 tablespoon regular soy sauce	) refrigerated.
1 tablespoon oil (optional)	)

¾ - 1 pound mung bean sprouts Washed. Discard soft discolored sprouts and bean shells that float to the surface. Drained.

1 medium onion Thinly sliced

1 rib celery Thinly sliced or shredded

1 carrot Peeled. Thinly sliced or shredded

1 scallion Thinly sliced

1 tablespoon fermented black beans

2 - 3 cloves garlic Minced.

¼ - 1 teaspoon Asian chili sauce

1½ teaspoons kosher salt or to taste

4 - 5 tablespoons oil

(1) Heat wok. Add 1 tablespoon oil. Swirl to coat wok. Add 1 teaspoon salt, bean sprouts, onion, celery and carrot. Stir-fry over high heat until bean sprouts reach desired doneness. Remove to a plate and set aside.

(2) Add 1 tablespoon oil to wok. Heat to smoking. Add beef. Stir-fry over high heat until beef changes color. Remove to a plate and set aside.

(3) Add 1 - 2 tablespoons oil to wok. Add black beans, garlic and ½ teaspoon salt. Stir-fry over medium heat until fragrant. Stir in chili sauce. Add drained ho fun. Mix well. Add vegetables, beef and scallion. Mix well. Serve.

NOTE: Can microwave fresh ho fun on high, 2-4 minutes, instead of dropping into boiling water.
****

Practical Variation

CHICKEN HO FUN

Substitute: *½ pound boneless and skinless chicken meat* for the *beef*

½ tablespoon dark soy sauce for *part of the regular soy sauce*

1 pound bok choy, sliced, for the *bean sprouts*

My Students' Favorite Chinese Recipes, updated edition

STIR-FRY RICE CAKE

serves 3 - 6

8 - 10 ounces dried rice cake Soak at least 24 hours. (May soak up to 3 days in the refrigerator, changing water daily.)

½ pound lean pork Cut into thin bite-sized pieces.	)
	) Combine
1 tablespoon ginger wine, p. 16	) Marinate if time permits.
1 tablespoon regular soy sauce	) Can be done the day before and
1 tablespoon oil	) refrigerated.
1 teaspoon sugar	)

½ - 1 pound napa cabbage Cut into ½-inch wide pieces.

2 - 4 ounces snow peas Stringed

1 carrot Peel. Slant cut thinly

1 scallion Cleaned and sliced thinly

¼ - 1 teaspoon Asian chili sauce (optional)

2 cloves garlic Minced finely.

1 teaspoon kosher salt or to taste

½ cup chicken broth

4 - 5 tablespoons oil

(1) Heat wok. Add 1 - 2 tablespoons oil. Swirl to coat wok. Add garlic. Stir-fry over medium heat until lightly browned. Stir in chili sauce. Add pork. Stir-fry over high heat until pork is cooked. Remove to a plate and set aside.

(2) Add 1 tablespoon oil to wok. Add ½ teaspoon salt, cabbage, snow peas and carrot. Stir-fry over high heat until snow peas change color. Remove to a plate. Set aside.

(3) Add 2 tablespoons oil and ½ teaspoon salt to wok. Drain rice cake and add to wok. Stir-fry over medium-high heat, adding broth a little at a time during stir-frying to prevent rice cake from sticking. Continue stir-frying and adding broth until rice cake is soft and all the broth is used.

(4) Add pork, vegetables and scallion. Mix well. Adjust taste. Serve hot.

****

Practical Variation

STIR-FRY CURRIED CHICKEN RICE CAKE

Substitute: *½ pound boneless and skinless chicken meat* for the *pork*

Add: *1 - 4 teaspoons curry powder* same time as chili sauce, step (1).

RICE CAKE WITH FERMENTED BLACK BEANS
serves 3 - 6

8 - 10 ounces dried rice cake Soak at least 24 hours. (See page 61.)

½ pound lean beef Cut across the	)
grain into thin bite-sized pieces.	)
1 tablespoon ginger wine, p. 16	) Combine. Marinate if time
1 tablespoon regular soy sauce	) permits. Can be done the day
1 tablespoon oil	) before and refrigerated.
1 teaspoon cornstarch	)
1 teaspoon brown sugar	)

1 pound mung bean sprouts Wash. Discard soft discolored sprouts and bean shells that float to the surface. Drain well.

3 - 4 dried Chinese mushrooms Soak in water at least ½ hour to soften. Squeeze out excess water. Remove and discard stems. Shred caps.

½ - 1 carrot Peeled. Shredded.

1 cup 2-inch lengths Chinese chives or ***shredded scallion to taste***

1 tablespoon fermented black beans Rinsed and drained.

2 - 3 cloves garlic Finely minced.

1 teaspoon kosher salt or to taste

¼ - 1 teaspoon Asian chili sauce or to taste

½ cup chicken broth

4 - 5 tablespoons oil

(1) Heat wok. Add 1 tablespoon oil. Add salt and mushrooms. Stir-fry 1 minute. Add bean sprouts, carrot and chives. Stir-fry over high heat until bean sprouts reach desired doneness. Remove to a plate. Set aside.

(2) Add 1 tablespoon oil. Add black beans and garlic. Stir-fry over high heat 30 seconds. Add beef, stir-fry until cooked. Remove to a plate. Set aside.

(3) Add 2 tablespoons oil and chili sauce to wok. Drain rice cake and add to wok. Stir-fry over medium-high heat, adding broth a little at a time during stir-frying to prevent rice cake from sticking. Continue stir-frying and adding broth until rice cake is soft and all the broth is used.

(4) Add beef and vegetables. Mix well. Adjust taste. Serve hot.

****

Practical Variation

RICE CAKE WITH FERMENTED BLACK BEANS & SHRIMP
Substitute: ***½ - ¾ pound shelled and deviened shrimp*** for the ***beef***

CURRIED RICE STICKS WITH PORK

> *½ pound lean pork* Shredded) Combine
> *1½ teaspoons regular soy sauce*) Marinate if time permits.
> *2 teaspoons ginger wine,* p. 16) Can be done the day before and
> *dash of white pepper or to taste*) refrigerated.

3 - 4 dried Chinese mushrooms Soak in water at least ½ hour to soften. Squeeze out excess water. Remove and discard stems. Shred caps.

½ - 1 carrot Peeled. Shredded.

¾ - 1 pound mung bean sprouts Wash. Discard soft discolored sprouts and bean shells that float to the surface. Drain well.

½ pound dried rice sticks Rinsed and drained.

1 egg Lightly beaten.

1 scallion Thinly sliced.

1 teaspoon kosher salt or to taste

1 - 2 teaspoons curry powder or to taste

1 - 1½ cups chicken broth

4 - 6 tablespoons oil

(1) Heat wok. Add 1 tablespoon oil. Swirl to coat wok. Turn heat to high. Add beaten egg. Tilt and turn wok to form a thin egg-pancake. Remove. Shred.

(2) Add 1 - 2 tablespoons oil to wok. Heat on high to near smoking. Add pork. Stir-fry over high heat until color changes. Remove to a plate and set aside.

(3) Add 1 tablespoon oil to wok. Add mushrooms. Stir-fry 1 minute over high heat. Add carrot and bean sprouts. Stir-fry until bean sprouts reach desired doneness. Remove, including any liquid, to a plate and set aside.

(4) Add 2 tablespoons oil, curry and salt. Stir-fry 5 seconds over high heat.

(5) Add rice sticks. Stir-fry over medium-high heat. Adding broth a little at a time while stir-frying. Continue stir-frying and adding broth until broth is used and rice sticks are soft. (Add liquid, if any, on plate with vegetables, to the rice sticks.) Mix in egg, pork, vegetables and scallion. Serve hot.

NOTE: Stir-frying curry powder for a few seconds in a little hot oil helps to prevent curry related indigestion.

****

Practical Variation
CURRIED RICE STICKS WITH CHICKEN

Substitute: *½ pound boneless* and *skinless chicken breast* for the *pork*
1½ teaspoons mushroom soy sauce for the *regular soy sauce*

ANTS CLIMBING TREE

serves 3 - 6

1 3.5-ounce package bean threads Soak in warm water for 15 minutes. Cut into about 4-inch lengths.

½ pound lean ground pork	)
1 tablespoon ginger wine, p. 16	) Combine.
1 tablespoon bean sauce	) Can be done ahead
1 tablespoon regular soy sauce	) of time and refrig-
1 tablespoon dark or mushroom soy sauce	) erated.
1 teaspoon sugar	)

2 cloves garlic Minced.
½ - 2 teaspoons Asian chili sauce or to taste
1 - 2 tablespoons oil
3 scallions Thinly sliced.
2 cups chicken or pork broth

(1) Heat wok. Add oil. Swirl to coat wok. Add garlic. Stir-fry over high heat 10 seconds. Add pork and chili sauce. Stir-fry until color changes.

(2) Drain bean thread. Add to pork. Stir to mix well. Add broth. Bring to a boil. Cover and simmer until most of the broth is absorbed. Stir in scallions. Serve hot with rice.

NOTE: The finished dish may appear soupy at first, but the bean threads will absorb most of the liquid in no time.

****

Practical Variations

VEGETARIAN ANTS CLIMBING TREE

Substitute: *12 ounces frozen firm* or *extra-firm tofu* for the *ground pork*
Thaw, page 73, and crumble tofu.

ANTS CLIMBING TREE WITH MISO

Substitute: *½ pound ground turkey* for the *ground pork*
1 - 3 tablespoons miso for the *bean sauce*

64 Noodles & Dough   My Students' Favorite Chinese Recipes, updated edition

CHINESE PANCAKE

makes 16 - 18 pancakes

2 cups unbleached flour
¾ - 1 cup boiling water
sesame oil or vegetable oil

(1) Measure flour into a mixing bowl. Make a well in the center of the flour. Pour boiling water into the well, stirring as you pour, using a pair of chopsticks or wooden spoon. Allow to cool for a few minutes.

(2) Turn dough on to a well floured surface. Knead until smooth and elastic, about 10 minutes. Cover with a damp towel. Let rest at least 30 minutes.

(3) Place an ungreased frying pan on range. Turn setting to medium low.

(4) Shape dough into a long sausage. Cut into 16 - 18 equal pieces.

(5) Flatten one piece of dough. Brush one side with a little sesame oil. Flatten another piece of dough. Place on top of oiled dough (oiled side) to form a sandwich. Using a rolling pin, roll sandwich-dough to a thin 7-inch diameter pancake.

(6) Place pancake in preheated frying pan. Cook over medium-low heat until puffed. Turn to cook the other side. Pancakes should not brown. Cool slightly, pull the 2 pancakes apart while still warm.

(7) Repeat with remaining dough.

To Serve: ❶ Ready steamer for steaming, page 15.

❷ Line steamer rack or steamer basket with a clean damp steaming towel or damp cheesecloth. Bring water to boil.

❸ Fold pancakes into ½'s or ¼'s. Place on top of damp towel, OK to overlap. Steam 5 - 10 minutes or until pliable.

KITCHEN HINT: Chinese pancakes freeze well. Cool. Stack. Package in freezer bag. Label, date and freeze. To serve: Steam, thawed or frozen.

KITCHEN HINT: To achieve a round pancake, place a 7-inch plate or a similar size pot cover on top of rolled, uncooked pancakes. Cut around the plate or cover. Uncover to find a round pancake.

My Students' Favorite Chinese Recipes, updated edition   Noodles & Dough **65**

HAM & SCALLION PANCAKE

makes 4

2 cups bread flour
¾ cup boiling water

2 tablespoons finely minced cooked ham	)
2 tablespoons finely minced scallion	) Combine.
1½ teaspoons kosher salt	)

2 tablespoons sesame oil (about)
½ cup vegetable oil (about)

(1) Measure flour into a mixing bowl. Make a well in the center of the flour. Pour boiling water into the well, stirring as you pour, using a pair of chopsticks or wooden spoon. Allow to cool for a few minutes.

(2) Turn dough on to a well floured surface. Knead until smooth and elastic, about 10 minutes. Cover with a damp towel. Let rest at least 30 minutes.

(3) Divide dough into 4 pieces. Roll one piece into a ⅛-inch thick circle. Brush liberally with sesame oil. Sprinkle ¼ of the ham mixture over the entire surface. Roll, jelly-roll style, into a long sausage. Shape into a coil, tucking under the exposed end. Press to flatten. Roll out into a ¼-inch thick circle.

(4) Heat a 10-inch or larger cast iron or heavy frying pan. Add 3 tablespoons oil. Heat over medium heat until oil is quite hot but not smoking. Slide a pancake into hot oil. Lower heat to medium low, cover and cook until pancake is golden, 2 - 4 minutes, shaking the frying pan every now and then to make pancake flaky.

(5) Turn pancake to brown the other side, adding more oil as needed. When both sides are browned, remove and drain on paper towel. Repeat with remaining pancakes. Cut into wedges. Serve hot or at room temperature.

****

Practical Variation

HAM & SCALLION QUESADILLAS

makes 8

Substitute: **8 10-inch flour tortillas** for the **dough**
Add: **1 cup shredded mozzarella cheese**
  4 tablespoons grated Parmesan cheese (optional)
  4 - 6 tablespoons butter Melted

❶ Add cheeses to ham mixture. Divide into 8 portions.

❷ Brush 1 tortilla liberally with **melted butter**. Place in ungreased frying pan, butter side down. Sprinkle 1 portion of ham and cheese mixture over ½ of the tortilla. Fold the other half over. Brown lightly, turn to brown other side.

My Students' Favorite Chinese Recipes, updated edition

EGGS

68
Egg Foo Yung

69
Steamed Eggs
Steamed Eggs with Beef

70
Steamed Eggs with Chinese Sausage

EGG RECIPES IN OTHER SECTIONS OF THIS BOOK

EGG FOO YUNG

serves 3 - 6

¼ pound raw shrimp Shelled. Deveined. Chopped coarsely

2 ounces roast pork or ham Shredded

4 - 6 dried Chinese mushrooms Soak in water at least ½ hour to soften.
   Squeeze out excess water. Remove and discard stems. Shred caps.

1 cup shredded bamboo shoots

1 tablespoon ginger wine, p. 16

1½ teaspoons kosher salt or to taste

4 - 5 white part of scallion Shredded or sliced thinly

6 extra large eggs Lightly beaten

¼ cup (about) oil for pan frying

¼ cup shredded green part of scallion

1 cup chicken broth	)
1 tablespoon regular soy sauce	) Combine in a small saucepan.
kosher salt to taste	) Stir well before bringing to boil.
2 teaspoons cornstarch	)

(1) Heat wok. Add 2 tablespoons oil. Swirl to coat wok. Add shrimp. Stir-fry over high heat until color changes. Add roast pork, mushrooms, bamboo shoots, ginger wine and salt. Stir-fry 1 minute. Stir in white part of scallion. Remove to a plate. Spread to cool. Up to this point can be done the day before and refrigerated.

(2) Add shrimp mixture to beaten eggs. Mix well.

(3) Heat a large frying pan. Add about ¼-inch of oil. Place as many metal egg rings in oil as frying pan will accommodate. Turn range to medium-high. When oil nears smoking pointing, pour ¼ - ⅓ cup egg mixture into each egg ring. Cook until egg is set and nicely browned at the bottom (adjust heat as needed.) Remove rings. Turn to brown the other side.

(4) Remove cooked egg foo yung to a warm serving platter. Repeat cooking if needed.

(5) Bring ingredients in saucepan to boil, stirring constantly until thickened. Spoon over egg foo yung. Garnish with green part of scallion. Serve.

KITCHEN HINT: Lacking egg rings? Make one big egg foo yung instead of small ones. Cut into wedges. Arrange wedges on serving platter.

STEAMED EGGS

6 extra large eggs Lightly beaten

2 large raw shrimp Shelled. Deveined. Diced or coarsely chopped.

1- 2 tablespoons chopped ham or other cooked meat

2 - 3 ounces coarsely ground chicken

2 dried Chinese mushrooms Soak in water at least ½ hour to soften.
   Squeeze out excess water. Remove and discard stems. Dice caps.

¼ cup frozen peas & carrots

1 tablespoon ginger wine, p. 16

1 teaspoon kosher salt or to taste

1½ cups chicken broth

1 scallion Cleaned. Shredded or sliced thinly, green and white parts.

¼ - ½ teaspoon Asian sesame oil

¾ cup chicken broth	) Combine in a small saucepan.
2 teaspoons cornstarch	) Stir well before bringing to a boil.
2 teaspoons regular soy sauce	)

(1) Brush a 10-inch glass pie plate or other heatproof deep dish with sesame oil.

(2) Combine eggs, shrimp, ham, chicken, mushrooms, peas & carrots, ginger wine and salt. Stir in 1½ cups broth. Pour into prepared heatproof dish.

(3) Steam (see page 15) over medium-low heat (225°-250°) for about 25 minutes or until knife inserted in the center comes out clean.

(4) Bring ingredients in saucepan to boil, stirring constantly until thickened. Spoon over steamed eggs. Sprinkle scallion on top. Serve hot with rice.

****

Practical Variation

STEAMED EGGS WITH BEEF

Substitute: **6 - 8 ounces extra lean ground beef** for the **shrimp, ham and chicken**

2 tablespoons mirim for the **ginger wine**

Add: **white pepper** to taste during step (2)

KITCHEN HINT: Steaming eggs at low temperature results in a soft, smooth texture. If your steamed eggs have a coarse porous texture, the heat was too high.

STEAMED EGGS WITH CHINESE SAUSAGE serves 3 - 6

6 extra large eggs Lightly beaten

2 Chinese sausage Shredded or sliced thinly

½ - 1 small carrot Shredded or chopped coarsely

3 - 4 dried Chinese mushrooms Soak in water at least ½ hour to soften.
   Squeeze out excess water. Remove and discard stems. Shred caps.

1 scallion Cleaned. Shredded or sliced thinly, green and white parts.

½ teaspoon kosher salt or to taste

1½ cups chicken broth

Chinese parsley for garnish

¼ - ½ teaspoon Asian sesame oil

¾ cup chicken broth	)
2 teaspoons cornstarch	) Combine in a small saucepan.
1 - 2 teaspoons oyster sauce	) Stir well before bringing to a boil.
1 tablespoon ginger wine, p. 16	)

(1) Brush a 10-inch glass pie plate or other heatproof deep dish with sesame oil.

(2) Combine eggs, sausage, carrot, mushrooms, scallion and salt. Stir in 1½ cups broth. Pour into prepared heatproof dish.

(3) Steam, page 15, over medium-low heat (225°-250°) for about 25 minutes or until knife inserted in the center comes out clean.

(4) Bring ingredients in saucepan to boil, stirring constantly. Spoon over steamed eggs. Garnish with parsley. Serve hot with rice.

TOFU, MEATLESS

ABOUT TOFU

Tofu, also known as **dow-foo**, **bean curd** and **soy cheese**, was discovered in China about 164 B.C.

Tofu is made by adding a coagulant to soy milk. After the coagulant is added, the soy milk separates into curds and whey. The curds are ladled into a cloth lined, perforated container. A cover and weight are placed directly on top of the curd. After about an hour, the curds will form a solid block of tofu. The most common coagulants used are magnesium chloride and calcium sulfate. Tofu made with calcium sulfate provides the highest amount of calcium.

Tofu, like the soybeans it is made from, is a complete protein. It contains all the essential amino acids making it an excellent meat substitute. High in calcium, it is low in fat and sodium, contains no cholesterol and is easy to digest.

The *useable protein content* of tofu is equivalent to chicken. This *useable protein content* increases when tofu is combined with meat, seafood, poultry, whole grain, dairy or nuts.

Tofu, marinated or plain, can be stir-fried, boiled, baked, deep fried or grilled. Tofu will take on the flavor of whatever it is cooked with and is happy with any meat, poultry, seafood or vegetables as its partner.

A highly perishable product, tofu should be stored in the same manner as dairy products. Buy only what you plan to use within a week. If you buy tofu in bulk, upon reaching home, transfer it from the cardboard container to a glass or plastic container, cover with cold water and place it in the refrigerator. Change the water daily. Use within a week. When buying pre-packaged tofu, check stamped date for freshness. Fresh tofu is bland. It should not smell or taste sour.

The varieties of tofu available are: silken, soft, firm, extra firm, 5-spiced and enriched. Silken tofu has the highest water content, has a smooth and custard-like texture. Extra firm tofu has the lowest water content. It is perfect for stir-frying. Tofu can be made firmer by wrapping in clean kitchen towel or layers of paper towels to remove the excess water.

One piece of soft tofu sold in bulk at the Chinese grocery store weighs approximately 8 ounces. One piece of the firm tofu sold in bulk weighs approximately 4 ounces. Pre-packaged tofu is one big block weighing 12 - 16 ounces.

Fresh tofu, in any form, can be frozen. Once frozen, fresh tofu changes from white to pale yellow. Thawed, it has a sponge-like texture.

ABOUT TOFU (continued)

To freeze tofu: Drain, place in a freezer bag. Label, date and freeze. Allow to freeze at least 24 hours before using. Frozen tofu will keep up to 6 months.

To thaw frozen tofu: Thaw in the refrigerator or place frozen tofu in a heat-proof container, cover with boiling water. Let stand until thawed, 15 or more minutes depending on the thickness of the frozen tofu. Gently press out the excess water. Use as directed in recipes.

One can also purchase **deep fried tofu**, also known as **tofu puffs**, **abura-age** and **atsu-age**, at the Asian markets. These are golden cubes (about 1½-inches) or slices that are very light weight.

Deep fried tofu, is fresh tofu that was deep fried. During deep-frying most of the water in the fresh tofu was extracted. The resulting product is a golden exterior and somewhat hollow interior.

Deep fried tofu is a very versatile product that makes an excellent meat substitute in braising, stir-frying or in soup. Can be used whole or cut into desired shapes or sizes. Deep fried tofu has a pleasant meaty texture and takes on the flavor of the foods with which it is cooked.

To make deep fried tofu in the home:
❶ Cut fresh tofu into 1-inch cubes or ½-inch thick slices or other desired sizes.
❷ Place, in one layer, on 2 - 3 thicknesses of dry clean kitchen towels or paper towels. Cover with another dry clean towel. Let stand 1 - 2 hours or until most of the moisture has been released, changing towels as needed.
❸ Heat oil for deep frying. Deep fry at 325° - 400° degrees for 12 - 15 minutes or until golden brown on all sides. (Lower tofu into hot oil one at a time to prevent pieces from sticking together.)
❹ Drain on paper towels. Deep fried tofu freezes well. Cool. Package in freezer bag. Date. Label. Freeze. Will keep up to 3 months.

Commercial deep fried tofu is made from specially prepared fresh tofu. The result is a very airy and honeycomblike inside. Homemade deep fried tofu is not quite as airy but is just as delicious.

Another method of frying tofu is to deep fry fresh soft tofu in very hot oil, 425°, for just a few minutes or until golden. This sears the tofu, making it crispy on the

ABOUT TOFU (continued)

outside while the inside remains soft and custardy.

Tofu is also available in a firmer cheese-like consistency, known as ***pressed tofu***. Pressed tofu is made by placing weight on fresh tofu to press out most of the water. The resulting product has a texture almost like mozzarella cheese.

Shredded pressed tofu looks like white rubber bands. It is available in 8-ounce bags and is known as ***kan ssu***.

Five-spice pressed tofu is pressed tofu seasoned with soy sauce and 5-spice powder. It is also available with chili peppers. Its color varies from light brown to dark brown. Five-spice pressed tofu can be purchased by the piece weighing 4 ounces each or in bags weighing 8 ounces. The thickness of the prepackaged pressed tofu varies and are interchangeable. Shredded 5-spice pressed tofu is available in 8-ounce bags.

Five-spiced pressed tofu can be eaten as is, add to salad or use in stir-fry. To store, keep in plastic bag and refrigerate (do not immerse in water.) Will keep up to a week. Do not use five-spice pressed tofu that smells sour, feels slimy or has a green appearance.

Another form of tofu, ***dried bean curd*** also known as ***tofu skin, bean curd skin, bean curd stick*** or ***yuba,*** is really not tofu in the true sense. Dried bean curd did not go through the process of coagulation as tofu did.

Dried bean curd is made from the sheet of thin film that forms on top of soy milk. This thin film was dried into flat sheets or formed into sticks (before drying.) Both are interchangeable in recipes. Soak in water for 2 hours to soften before using in recipes.

Because of its high fat content, dried bean curd will become rancid if kept too long on the pantry shelf. Store no longer than 3 months. For longer storage, up to a year, keep in freezer.

SOY BEAN SPROUTS BROTH

makes 3 - 4 cups

1 pound soy bean sprouts Discard any shells and blackened beans. Washed.
   Drained. Chopped coarsely.
2 slices fresh ginger
2 - 3 peppercorns
1 small carrot Thinly sliced or coarsely chopped
1 scallion Leave whole or cut into 2 or 3 sections
1 teaspoon kosher salt or to taste
1 tablespoon oil
4 - 5 cups water

(1) Heat stock pot. Add oil and ginger slices. When ginger slices begin to brown
    slightly, add salt and chopped bean sprouts. Stir-fry until bean sprouts will
    not release any more liquid, about 5 minutes.

(2) Add peppercorns, carrot, scallion and water. Bring to boil. Simmer 1 hour.

(3) Strain broth through a fine strainer or two layers of dampened cheesecloth.
    Use in place of meat broth in recipes.

KITCHEN HINT: Double or triple recipe if a stock pot is large enough to accommodate all the
              ingredients.
KITCHEN HINT: Freeze cooled broth in ice cube trays. Once frozen, remove from ice cube tray.
              Store in freezer bags or freezer containers. Label, date and return to freezer.
              Use as needed. Will keep up to 6 months. Make a note of how many table-
              spoons of liquid each broth cube contains.
              For individual servings, freeze cooled broth in muffin pans. Once frozen,
              remove from muffin pans. Store in freezer bags or freezer containers. Label,
              date and return to freezer.

****

About soy bean sprouts

Soy bean sprouts play an important role in the part of meatless cooking. Soy bean
sprouts, like the soy beans from which they are grown, are high in protein. After
sprouting, the carbohydrate in the soy beans is converted into vitamins C and B.

Soy beans sprouts are available in Chinese grocery stores, health food stores and
some supermarkets. Always cook soy bean sprouts before eating.

SOY BEAN SPROUTS SOUP

½ pound soy bean sprouts Discard any shells and blackened beans. Washed. Drained. Chopped coarsely.

2 slices fresh ginger

1 small carrot Diced

2 - 3 dried Chinese mushrooms Soak in water at least ½ hour to soften. Squeeze out excess water. Remove and discard stems. Dice caps.

1 scallion Thinly sliced or shredded

½ teaspoon kosher salt or to taste

2 teaspoons oil

¼ - ½ teaspoon Asian sesame oil

white pepper to taste

Asian chili oil or *Asian chili sauce to taste* (optional)

3 - 4 cups water

(1) Heat stock pot. Add oil and ginger slices. When ginger slices begin to brown slightly, add salt and chopped bean sprouts. Stir-fry 2 - 4 minutes or until bean sprouts are wilted.

(2) Add carrot, mushrooms and water. Bring to boil. Cover. Simmer 30 - 45 minutes. Stir in sesame oil and scallion. Add white pepper and chili oil to taste. Serve hot.

****

Practical Variations

TOFU SOY BEAN SPROUTS SOUP

Add: *4 - 6 ounces soft* or *firm tofu* Cut tofu into small cubes or thin slices. Add during step (2).

PORK & SOY BEAN SPROUTS SOUP

Add: *1 - 2 pounds pork bone* or *spareribs* during step (2)
   1 - 2 additional cups of water
   Simmer 1 - 1½ hours.

EGG FLOWER SOUP

4 - 6 cups vegetable broth
1 - 2 onions Thinly sliced
2 tomatoes Peeled. Remove and discard seeds. Cut into ⅛'s.
2 - 4 ounces soft tofu (optional) Cut into about ¼-inch cubes or thinly sliced.
1 egg Lightly beaten
2 - 3 tablespoons oil
kosher salt to taste
white pepper to taste
Chinese parsley or *regular parsley for garnish* (optional)

(1) Heat wok or small frying pan. Add oil. Stir-fry onions over medium to medium high heat until golden.
(2) Place broth in a large pot. Drain onions and add to broth. Bring to boil. Add tomatoes, tofu and white pepper. Bring to boil. Simmer about 1 minute.
(3) Gently stir broth while slowly adding beaten egg. Add salt to taste. Ladle into individual soup bowls. Garnish with parsley. Serve hot.

KITCHEN HINT: Chicken broth may be substituted for the vegetable broth.

****

CORN & TOFU CHOWDER

3 - 4 cups vegetable broth
1 14-ounce can cream-style corn
8 ounces soft or *silken tofu* Mashed with a fork
2 egg whites or *1 whole egg* Lightly beaten
¼ - ½ teaspoon Asian sesame oil or to taste
Asian chili oil or *chili sauce to taste* (optional)
1 - 2 tablespoons thinly sliced green part of scallion

(1) In a stockpot, bring broth to boil. Add tofu, bring to boil using medium heat.
(2) Add corn. Bring to boil. Stir in egg whites or whole egg then sesame oil.
(3) Ladle into individual serving bowls. Garnish with scallion and a drop or 2 of chili oil, if using. Serve hot.

MEATLESS FRIED WONTONS

6 (about 1 ounce) Chinese deep fried tofu Cover with hot water. Gently squeeze to remove excess oil. Rinse in warm water. Squeeze dry. Coarsely chopped.

¼ cup coarsely chopped water chestnuts	)
1 scallion Thinly sliced.	) Combine. Mix in
3 - 5 dried Chinese mushrooms Soak in water to	) tofu. This is the
soften. Squeeze dry. Discard stems. Chop caps	) wonton filling.
¼ teaspoon sugar	) Can be done the
1 tablespoon ginger wine, p. 16	) day before and
1 tablespoon oyster sauce	) refrigerated.
1 egg Lightly beaten	)

½ - ¾ pound ready-made wonton wrappers (about 45)
oil for deep frying

2 tablespoons ketchup	) Combine in a small serving
1 teaspoon Asian sesame oil	) bowl.
¼ - 1 teaspoon Asian chili sauce	) This is the sauce.

(1) Assemble wontons as per instructions on page 21. Place on a dry plate. Cover with a clean damp kitchen towel.

(2) Deep fry at 375° until golden, about 2 minutes. Drain on paper towels. Serve warm or at room temperature with or without sauce.

****

Practical Variation

MEATLESS WONTON SOUP

❶ Assemble wontons as per instructions on page 33, using the meatless fried wontons filling above. Place assembled wontons on a dry plate and cover with a dry towel

❷ Follow cooking instruction (2) and (3) on page 32.

FROZEN TOFU FRIED RICE

serves 3 - 6

4 cups cooked white or *brown rice* Cooled and fluffed.

8 - 12 ounces frozen tofu Thawed, p. 73. Squeeze out excess water.
Crumbled or coarsely chopped.

3 eggs Lightly beaten

¾ cup frozen green soy beans Thawed

1 carrot Peeled. Coarsely chopped

2 - 4 dried Chinese mushrooms Soak in water at least 30 minutes to soften.
Squeeze out excess water. Discard stems. Chop caps coarsely.

¼ cup chopped onion

1 - 2 cloves garlic Minced

1 - 2 scallion Thinly sliced

1 teaspoon kosher salt or to taste

2 - 3 tablespoons dark or *mushroom soy sauce*

3 - 4 tablespoons oil

1 - 2 teaspoons Asian sesame oil (optional)

(1) Heat wok. Add 1 tablespoon oil. Swirl to coat wok. Heat to near smoking.
Add eggs. Scramble until just set. Remove to a plate. Cut into small pieces.

(2) Add 1 tablespoon oil to wok. Add soy beans, carrot and mushrooms. Stir-fry
over high heat until mushrooms are fragrant. Remove to a plate.

(3) Add 1 - 2 tablespoons oil to wok. Add onion and garlic. Stir-fry over
medium high heat until onion is lightly browned. Add tofu and 1 tablespoon
soy sauce. Stir-fry until tofu is browned.

(4) Add salt and rice. Stir-fry over high to medium high heat until rice is heated.
Add remaining soy sauce to taste. Stir-fry until rice is evenly coated with soy
sauce.

(5) Add vegetables, scallion, scrambled eggs and sesame oil. Stir-fry until everything is heated through. Serve hot.

****

Practical Variation

CURRIED FROZEN TOFU FRIED RICE

Substitute: *½ cup each diced red pepper, broccoli florets* and *cauliflower*
for the *carrot* and *mushrooms*

Add: *1 - 3 teaspoons curry powder* during step (3)

MUSHROOM FRIED RICE

serves 3 - 6

4 cups cooked white rice Cooled and fluffed.

4 - 6 dried Chinese mushrooms Soak in water at least 30 minutes to soften. Squeeze out excess water. Discard stems. Dice or coarsely chop caps.

2 - 2½ ounces Chinese deep fried tofu Cover with hot water. Gently squeeze to remove excess oil. Rinse in warm water. Squeeze dry. Coarsely chopped.

3 eggs Lightly beaten

¾ cup fresh or *frozen green peas*

1 carrot Diced or coarsely chopped

1 - 2 scallions Thinly sliced

1 teaspoon kosher salt or to taste

1 - 2 tablespoons mushroom soy sauce

1 - 2 tablespoons toasted sesame seeds

3 - 4 tablespoons oil

3 - 4 tablespoons broth or *water*

1 - 2 teaspoons Asian sesame oil (optional)

(1) Heat wok. Add 1-2 tablespoons oil. Swirl to coat wok. Heat to near smoking. Add eggs. Scramble until just set. Remove to a plate. Cut into small pieces.

(2) Add 1 tablespoon oil to wok. Add mushrooms. Stir fry over high heat until mushrooms are fragrant, 1 - 2 minutes. Add peas and carrot. Stir-fry another 2 minutes, adding broth or water 1 tablespoon at a time if wok is dry. Remove to a plate.

(3) Add 1 tablespoon oil to wok. Add salt and rice. Stir-fry over high to medium high heat until rice is coated with oil. Add soy sauce. Stir-fry until rice is evenly coated with soy sauce.

(4) Add tofu. Stir-fry until tofu is heated through.

(5) Add vegetables, scallion, scrambled eggs, sesame seeds and sesame oil. Stir-fry until everything is heated through. Serve hot.

****

Practical Variation

PORTABELLA PINEAPPLE FRIED RICE

Substitute: ***Cooked brown rice*** for the ***white rice***

8 ounces portabella mushrooms for the ***Chinese mushrooms***
Cut portabella into about ½-inch cubes.

½ cup each red, green and ***yellow pepper*** for the ***peas*** and ***carrot***

Add: ***½ cup pineapple tidbits*** during step (5)

FROZEN TOFU, NUTS & VEGETABLES   serves 3 - 6

12 - 16 ounces frozen firm or *extra firm tofu* Thawed, p. 73. Squeeze out excess water. Cut into about ½-inch cubes.

½ teaspoon sugar	) Combine.
1 tablespoon ginger wine, p. 16	) Add tofu. Mix well.
2 teaspoons regular soy sauce	) Can be done the day
2 teaspoons dark or *mushroom soy sauce*	) before and refrigerated.

1 - 2 dried or *fresh chili peppers (optional)* Discard seeds. Thinly slice pods.
1 clove garlic Minced
2 - 3 tablespoons oil
¾ cup frozen peas & carrots
1 small onion Cut to size of peas
¼ - ½ cup diced bamboo shoots
1 teaspoon kosher salt or to taste
1 cup broth or *water*
½ - 1 cup roasted unsalted cashew or *other nuts*
1 scallion Thinly sliced

1 teaspoon cornstarch	) Combine in a small bowl.
1 tablespoon broth or *water*	) Stir well just before adding to wok.

(1) Heat wok. Add oil. Swirl to coat wok. Add chili peppers and garlic. Stir-fry over high heat 10 seconds. Add tofu. Stir-fry until lightly browned.

(2) Add salt and vegetables. Stir-fry over high heat about 1 minute Add broth. Mix well. Bring to a boil. Cover and simmer until vegetables reach desired doneness, 2 - 3 minutes.

(3) Thicken with cornstarch mixture. Stir in nuts. Remove to serving platter. Sprinkle scallion on top. Serve hot.

****

Practical Variation

FROZEN TOFU WITH PORTABELLA & ZUCCHINI

Cut: *frozen tofu* into thin slices instead of cubes.

Substitute: *4 - 8 ounces sliced portabella mushrooms* for the *peas & carrots*

4 - 6 ounces sliced zucchini for the *bamboo shoots*

MEATLESS CABBAGE ROLLS

serves 3 - 6

12 ounces frozen firm or extra firm tofu Thawed, p. 73. Crumbled.

¾ teaspoon kosher salt or to taste)	
¼ teaspoon sugar)	
dash of white or *black pepper*)	Combine in a mixing bowl.
1 tablespoon cornstarch)	Add crumbled tofu.
1 tablespoon ginger wine, p. 16)	Mix well.
1 tablespoon dark soy sauce)	Divide into 15 portions.
4 ounces onion Minced)	
1 egg Lightly beaten)	

2 tablespoons sugar)	
2 tablespoons white vinegar)	Combine in a small saucepan.
1 tablespoon regular soy sauce)	This is the sauce.
1 cup liquid from steamed cabbage)	
roll or *broth* or *combination*)	

1 tablespoon cornstarch)	Combine in a small dish.
2 tablespoons water)	Stir well just before adding to saucepan.

15 napa cabbage leaves Cut leafy sections into 5- or 6-inch lengths. Save stem sections for another use. Blanch leafy sections for 2 minutes. Drain and cool under cold running water. Drain again well.

(1) Assemble cabbage roll as per instructions. Arrange on a 10-inch pyrex dish or other heat-proof deep dish. Steam over high heat for 15 minutes.

(2) Bring sauce to a boil. Thicken with cornstarch mixture. Spoon over rolls.

Assembling cabbage rolls

❶ Place 1 portion filling near cut end of cabbage leaf.   ❷ Fold leaf, cut end, over filling.   ❸ Fold over both left and right sides.   ❹ Roll.

LOUHAN JAI

2 folded sheets dried bean curd *(flat type)* Soak in water about 1 hour to soften. Cut into about ½-inch x 2-inch strips.

¼ cup tiger lily flowers Soak in water at least ½ hour to soften. Remove and discard any hard and woody parts. Tie each into a knot (optional).

1- 2 tablespoons cloud ears Soak in water at least ½ hour to soften. Remove and discard any sandy and woody parts. Break into small pieces.

½ - 1 14-ounce can straw mushrooms Rinsed. Drained.

½ pound asparagus Peeled. Remove scales, p. 99. Slant-cut into about ½-inch thick slices.

¼ pound snow peas Stringed

1 carrot Peeled. Slant-cut into about ¼-inch thick slices.

¾ pound napa cabbage Cut into about ½ - ¾-inch thick strips.

2 tablespoons oil

1 teaspoon kosher salt or **to taste**

½ teaspoon sugar

¼ teaspoon white or **black pepper or to taste**

3 - 4 tablespoons oyster sauce

1½ cups chicken broth

1 tablespoon cornstarch	) Combine in a small bowl.
2 tablespoons broth or **water**	) Stir well just before adding to wok.

(1) Heat wok. Add 1 tablespoon oil. Swirl to coat wok. Add salt, asparagus and snow peas. Stir-fry over high heat until snow peas change color. Remove to a plate.

(2) Add 1 tablespoon oil to wok. Add carrot and cabbage. Stir-fry over high heat 1 minute. Add tiger lily, cloud ears and straw mushrooms. Stir-fry 1 minute. Add bean curd, sugar and pepper. Mix well. Add broth. Bring to boil. Cover. Simmer 10 minutes.

(3) Add asparagus, snowpeas and oyster sauce. Mix well. Thicken with corn-starch mixture. Serve hot.

****

Practical Variation

LOUHAN JAI WITH FRESH TOFU

Substitute: ***1 pound extra-firm or firm tofu*** for the ***dried bean curd*** Cut tofu into ¼-inch thick bite-size slices.

5-SPICED PRESSED TOFU STIR-FRY serves 3 - 6

8 ounces 5-spiced pressed tofu Thinly sliced or shredded
1 rib celery Slant cut thinly or shredded
1 carrot Slant cut thinly or shredded
¾ cup sliced or *shredded bamboo shoot*
4 - 6 dried Chinese mushrooms Soak in water at least ½ hour to soften.
   Squeeze out excess water. Remove and discard stems. Slice caps thinly.
2 - 3 scallions Thinly sliced
2 tablespoons oil
¼ teaspoon kosher salt or to taste
1 teaspoon sugar
white or *black pepper to taste*
1 tablespoon oyster sauce
1 - 2 tablespoons broth or *water*

2 teaspoons cornstarch)	Combine in a small bowl.
1 tablespoon water)	Stir well just before adding to wok.

Pita bread halves Steamed, p. 149, or unsteamed
Leaf lettuce

(1) Heat wok. Add oil. Swirl to coat wok. Add salt and mushrooms. Stir-fry over high heat until fragrant 1 - 2 minutes. Stir in tofu.

(2) Add all vegetables, sugar, pepper and oyster sauce. Stir-fry about 2 minutes or until vegetables reach desired doneness. Add broth or water 1 tablespoon at a time if wok is dry.

(3) Thicken with cornstarch mixture. Stir in scallion. Remove to serving platter.

To serve: Place a piece of lettuce leaf in pita half. Fill with tofu mixture and enjoy.

****

Practical Variation

5-SPICED PRESSED TOFU TORTILLA ROLLS

Substitute: *Flour tortilla* for the *pita*
        Wrap tortilla in aluminum foil. Place in 300° oven for 10 minutes to soften. Place a piece of lettuce on center of tortilla. Top with some tofu mixture. Roll and enjoy.

TOFU COMBINED WITH MEAT

TOFU VEGETABLE SOUP

serves 3 - 6

8 ounces soft tofu Cut into small cubes or coarsely mash with a fork.

2 - 4 ounces Chinese roast pork, ham or **other cooked meat** Sliced thinly or shredded.

6 raw shrimp Shelled. Deveined. Cut in halves, lengthwise, or leave whole.

---

1 - 2 pounds vegetables Use any of the following vegetables alone or in combination or choose others.

Carrot Cut into about ¼-inch thick slices.

Zucchini Cut into about ¼-inch thick slices.

Mushroom Cut into about ¼-inch thick slices.

Snow peas Stringed and washed.

Bok choy Washed well. Cut into about ¼-inch thick slices.

Napa cabbage Cut into about ½-inch thick slices

---

1 scallion Cleaned. Shredded or sliced thinly.

4 cups broth

½ teaspoon Asian sesame oil (optional)

few drops chili oil (optional)

2 - 3 slices ginger

(1) In large pot, bring broth to boil. Add carrot. Simmer 1 minute.

(2) Add shrimp, ginger and remaining vegetables. Bring to boil. Simmer 2 minutes or until vegetables reach desired doneness.

(3) Add cooked meat and tofu. Bring to boil. Stir in scallion, sesame oil and chili oil, if using. Serve hot.

****

Practical Variation

TOFU VEGETABLE SOUP WITH EGGS

Substitute: **3 - 6 eggs** (1 per person) for the **roast pork** Crack eggs, 1 at a time, directly into simmering broth during step (1).

HOT & SOUR SOUP

serves 3 - 6

2 - 4 ounces lean pork Shredded)	
¼ teaspoon cornstarch)	Combine and marinate. Can be
1 teaspoon ginger wine, p. 16)	done the day before. Refrigerated.
1 teaspoon regular soy sauce)	

3 - 6 dried Chinese mushrooms Soak in water at least ½ hour to soften. Squeeze out excess water. Remove and discard stems. Shred caps.

20 tiger lily flowers Soak in water at least ½ hour to soften. Remove and discard any hard and woody parts. Cut in half.

1 tablespoon cloud ears Soak in water at least ½ hour to soften. Remove and discard any sandy and woody parts. Break into small pieces.

¼ cup shredded bamboo shoots

8 - 16 ounces soft tofu Cut into thin strips

1 tablespoon regular soy sauce

¼ - 1 teaspoon Asian chili sauce or to taste

¼ teaspoon white pepper or to taste

1 teaspoon kosher salt or to taste

4 tablespoons white vinegar or to taste

1 egg Lightly beaten

2 teaspoons sesame oil

1 scallion Cleaned. Shredded or sliced thinly.

1 sheet dried laver Torn into small pieces (optional)

1- 2 tablespoons shredded ja choy (Szechuan preserved vegetables) (optional)

2 tablespoons cornstarch)	Combine in a small bowl.
3 tablespoons water)	Stir well just before adding to pot.

(1) In a large pot bring broth to boil over high heat. Add mushrooms, cloud ears, tiger lily flowers, bamboo shoots and pork. Bring to boil. Stir in white pepper, chili sauce and soy sauce.

(2) Add tofu. Add laver and ja choy (if using). Bring to boil over medium heat. Stir in vinegar. Gently stir soup while slowly adding cornstarch mixture. Continue stirring and slowly add beaten egg.

(3) Remove from heat. Stir in sesame oil, scallion and salt to taste. Serve hot.

KITCHEN HINT: For a meatless version, omit pork.

CHICKEN TOFU DUMPLING SOUP serves 3 - 6

4 ounces soft tofu Place in a clean, dry kitchen towel. Squeeze out as much
water as possible. Crumbled.

2 ounces chicken meat Minced	)
1 tablespoon finely minced white part of scallion	)
½ teaspoon kosher salt or to taste	) Combine.
pinch of sugar	) Add crumbled
dash of white pepper or to taste	) tofu. Mix
1½ teaspoons cornstarch	) well.
½ of an egg white Lightly beaten	)
¼ teaspoon sesame Asian oil	)

4 - 6 cups chicken broth
2 - 4 ounces snow peas Stringed
½ - 1 carrot Thinly sliced
½ - 1 small zucchini Sliced
½ can straw mushrooms Leave whole or cut in halves.
green part of scallion Sliced or shredded.

(1) In large saucepan, bring broth to boil. Lower range to maintain a slow
    simmer. Drop chicken-tofu mixture by teaspoonful into simmering broth.
    Simmer gently for 5 minutes.
(2) Add vegetables. Bring to a boil. Simmer about 2 minutes or until vegetables
    reach desired doneness.
(3) Sprinkle on scallion green. Serve hot.

****

Practical Variation

SEAFOOD TOFU DUMPLING SOUP

Substitute: ***2 ounces raw shrimp*** or ***2 ounces sea scallops*** for the ***chicken***
       1 angled luffa for the ***zucchini***
Add: ***1 1.7-ounce bag bean thread*** Soak bean thread in warm water for
       15 minutes. Cut into shorter lengths. Add to broth during step (2).
       1 - 2 teaspoons Chinese red vinegar or to taste during step (3).
       ¼ - 1 teaspoon Asian chili sauce or to taste during step (3).

STEAMED TOFU MEATBALLS

serves 3 - 6

1 cup glutinous rice Soak for 2 hours. Drained.

8 ounces firm or *extra firm tofu* Cut into 2 or 3 large chunks. Place in colander. Drain 30 minutes. Mash with a fork.

½ pound lean ground pork

3 - 5 dried Chinese mushrooms Soak in water at least 30 minutes to soften. Squeeze out excess water. Remove and discard stems. Finely chop caps.

1 - 2 pounds napa cabbage or *green cabbage* Sliced thinly.

1 whole egg or *2 egg whites* Lightly beaten	) Combine in a large
½ teaspoon kosher salt or to taste	) bowl. Add tofu, pork
2 teaspoons Asian sesame oil	) and mushrooms.
2 tablespoons tapioca starch or *cornstarch*	) Shape into meat-
1 tablespoon ginger wine, p. 16	) balls, using about 1
2 tablespoons oyster sauce	) tablespoon mixture.
3 tablespoons minced water chestnuts	) Roll into drained
1 scallion Minced	) rice. Repeat.

2 tablespoons regular soy sauce	) Combine in
2 tablespoons Chinese red vinegar or *malt vinegar*	) a small
¼ - ½ teaspoon Asian chili sauce (optional)	) serving bowl
½ teaspoon Asian sesame oil	) for sauce.

(1) Line steamer rack or steamer basket with cabbage. Steam for 5 - 10 minutes or until soften.

(2) Place meatballs, in one layer on top of softened cabbage, leaving a little space between each. Steam covered, over high heat for 30 minutes. Serve hot with sauce.

****

Practical Variation

Substitute: *½ pound ground chicken, ground turkey, ground beef* or *ground veal* for the *ground pork*

NOODLES WITH TOFU MEAT SAUCE   serves 3 - 6

½ pound lean ground pork or *beef*

12 - 16 ounces frozen tofu, p. 73 Thawed. Crumbled or coarsely chopped.

6 - 8 cloves garlic Peeled. Minced.

5 - 6 scallions Cleaned. Sliced thinly. Reserve 1 - 2 tablespoons green part for garnish.

1 tablespoon ginger wine, p. 16

1 tablespoon dark soy sauce

2 - 3 tablespoons bean sauce

1 teaspoon honey

2 tablespoons oil

1 cup chicken or *vegetable broth*

1 teaspoon cornstarch)	Combine in a small bowl.
1 tablespoon water)	Stir well just before adding to wok.

1 pound fresh Chinese egg noodles

2 teaspoons sesame oil or vegetable oil (optional)

1 - 2 cucumbers Peeled. Shredded or sliced thinly.

(1) Heat wok. Add oil, garlic and scallion. Stir-fry over medium heat for about 30 seconds. Add ground pork. Stir-fry over high heat until color changes.

(2) Add crumbled frozen tofu. Stir-fry over high heat for about 2 minutes. Stir in ginger wine, dark soy sauce, bean sauce and honey. Mix well.

(3) Add broth. Bring to boil. Cover. Simmer 5 minutes. Thicken with cornstarch mixture. Transfer to a serving bowl. Sprinkle reserved scallion on top.

(4) While tofu meat sauce is cooking, bring a large pot of water to boil. Add noodles. Cook, uncovered, over medium high heat for 6 minutes. Drain. Place on a preheated serving platter or serving bowl. Toss with sesame oil.

To serve: Place a portion of noodles on a plate, top with some cucumber and tofu meat sauce.

****

Practical Variation

ROTINI WITH MEATLESS SAUCE

Substitute: *6 - 8 ounces rotini* for the *egg noodles* Cook rotini according to package directions.

8 - 12 ounces frozen green soy beans for the *ground pork* Thaw soy beans. Add frozen tofu during step (1), add green soy beans during step (3).

TOFU STIR-FRY

1 pound extra-firm or *firm tofu* Cut into ¾-inch cubes or ¼-inch thick slices
4 ounces Chinese roast pork or *smoked ham* Thinly sliced
1 stalk broccoli Peel stem. Cut into bite-size pieces. Cut florets into bite-size
pieces. Blanched, p. 100.
1 carrot Peeled and slant cut
4 ounces fresh mushrooms Washed. Cut into ¼-inch thick slices.
1 small onion Peeled. Cut into small wedges.
1 clove garlic Peeled. Minced.
3 - 4 tablespoons oil
1 teaspoon kosher salt or to taste
3 - 4 tablespoons broth or as needed

1 teaspoon cornstarch	) Combine in a small
2 teaspoons oyster sauce	) bowl for sauce.
1 tablespoon ginger wine, p. 16	) Stir well just before
2 tablespoons broth	) adding to wok.
¼ teaspoon Asian chili sauce or to taste	)

(1) Heat wok. Add 1 tablespoon oil. Swirl to coat wok. Add salt, broccoli, carrot,
    mushrooms and onion. Stir-fry over high heat for 2 minutes or until reached
    desired doneness, adding broth 1 tablespoon at a time if wok is dry. Remove
    to a plate. Set aside.

(2) Add 1 tablespoon oil to wok. Add garlic. Stir-fry over high heat 10 seconds.
    Add pork. Stir-fry 30 seconds. Remove to a plate. Set aside.

(3) Add 1 - 2 tablespoons oil to wok. Heat until near smoking. Add tofu. Stir-fry,
    gently, over high heat until heated through, 2 - 3 minutes.

(4) Add vegetables and pork. Mix well. Stir in sauce. Bring to boil. Serve hot.
****

Practical Variation

FIVE-SPICED TOFU STIR-FRY

1 tablespoon mushroom or	) Combine. Add tofu (above). Mix gently
dark soy sauce	) to coat each piece. Can be done the
¼ teaspoon 5-spice powder	) day before and refrigerated.
½ teaspoon sugar	) All remaining ingredients and cooking
1 tablespoon ginger wine	) instructions remain the same.

TOFU BURGER & MUSHROOM SAUCE   serves 3 - 6

½ pound extra lean ground beef

8 ounces soft or *firm tofu* Cut into 2 or 3 large chunks. Place in a colander to drain for 30 minutes. Mash with a fork.

8 ounces red skin or other *all purpose potato* Peeled. Shred using a food processor or a box grater.

1 egg Lightly beaten	)
1 small onion Minced or finely diced	) Combine in a large bowl.
1 clove garlic Finely minced or pureed	) Add potato. Mix well.
1½ tablespoons cornstarch	) Add tofu. Mix well.
1 tablespoon oyster sauce	) Add beef. Mix to just
1 tablespoon ketchup	) combine.
¼ teaspoon black pepper or to taste	) Shape into 6 - 8 burgers,
½ teaspoon sugar	) about ½-inch thick.
½ teaspoon kosher salt or to taste	)

parsley for garnish (optional)
oil for pan frying
Mushroom Sauce, p. 93

(1) Make mushroom sauce.

(2) Heat a frying pan. Add about ¼-inch oil. Heat to near smoking. Pan-fry burgers until browned on both sides. Place browned burgers, single layer, on a 8 x 12 x 1½-inch pyrex dish or other heatproof deep serving dish.

(3) Spoon mushroom sauce over burgers. Bake uncovered in 350° preheated oven for 30 minutes, or until burgers are cooked through. Garnish with parsley and serve.

Alternative cooking method: ❶ Place shaped burgers, single layer, on a generously oiled 8 x 12 x 1½-inch pyrex dish or other heatproof deep serving dish.

❷ Bake uncovered, in 375° preheated oven, for 45 - 50 minutes or until cooked.

❸ Spoon mushroom sauce over cooked burgers. Garnish with parsley. Serve.

TOFU BURGER & MUSHROOM SAUCE (continued)

MUSHROOM SAUCE

3 - 4 dried Chinese mushrooms (*optional*) Soak at least 30 minutes to soften. Remove and discard stems. Chop caps finely.

4 ounces fresh mushrooms Coarsely chopped.

1 small onion Thinly sliced

1 clove garlic Minced

¼ teaspoon kosher salt or to taste

¼ teaspoon black pepper or to taste

¾ cup broth

1 - 2 tablespoons oil

1½ teaspoons cornstarch	) Combine in a small bowl.
1 tablespoon water	) Stir well just before adding to saucepan.

❶ Heat a small saucepan. Add oil and mushrooms. Stir-fry over medium-high heat for 5 minutes.

❷ Add broth. Bring to boil. Simmer 3 minutes. Thicken with cornstarch mixture.

Alternative serving methods: Serve burgers, without mushroom sauce, on a bun with lettuce, tomato, pickle, ketchup and/or mustard.

****

Practical Variation

TOFU TURKEY BURGER & MUSHROOM SAUCE

Substitute: *½ pound ground turkey* for the *ground beef*

1½ tablespoons flour for the *cornstarch*

TOFU POCKETS

¼ *pound lean ground pork*	)
¼ *pound raw shrimp* Shelled. Deveined.	)
Chopped finely.	) Combine. Mix
2 scallions, white part Minced or chopped finely	) well. This is the
¼ *teaspoon white pepper or to taste*	) stuffing.
½ *teaspoon kosher salt or to taste*	) Can be done the
2 teaspoons ginger wine, p. 16	) day before and
1 teaspoon regular soy sauce	) refrigerated.
1 teaspoon Asian sesame oil	)
½ *of a beaten egg*	)

1 pound firm tofu Drained.
    Cut into 16 triangles.
    See diagram at right.

oil for pan frying
½ *cup chicken broth* or *water*

2 teaspoons cornstarch	) Combine in a small bowl.
2 tablespoons water	) Stir well just before adding to
1½ *tablespoons oyster sauce*	) frying pan.
dash of white pepper or to taste	)

Green part of scallion Shredded or sliced thinly
Romaine lettuce (*optional*) Cut each leaf into 2 or 3 sections.

(1) Cut a slit along the long side of the triangle to form a pocket.

(2) Place about 1½ teaspoons stuffing in pocket. Repeat with other pieces.

(3) Heat a frying pan. Add about ¼-inch oil and heat until near smoking. Place stuffed tofu, meat side down in hot oil. Brown lightly. Brown other sides.

(4) Add broth. Bring to a boil. Cover and simmer 7 - 10 minutes or until meat is thoroughly cooked.

(5) While tofu is simmering, heat about 1 tablespoon oil in wok. Add ¼ - ½ teaspoon salt, add lettuce and stir-fry until just heated through, about 3 minutes. Drain and arrange on serving platter.

(6) Remove cooked tofu with a slotted spoon and arrange on top of cooked lettuce. Thicken gravy with cornstarch mixture. Spoon gravy over tofu. Sprinkle scallion green on top and serve.

KITCHEN HINT: Make small meatballs with leftover stuffing. Add to frying pan during step (4).

Practical Variations

STUFFED EGGPLANT

Substitute: *2 - 3 Chinese eggplant* for the *tofu*

❶ Slant cut a ½-inch thick slice of eggplant, cutting about ¾ of the way through.

❷ Cut another ½-inch thick slice, this time all the way through, resulting in a 1-inch thick, hinged, slice of eggplant.

❸ Repeat above 2 steps with remaining eggplant.

❹ Spread 1 - 2 teaspoons stuffing in the center cut to make a sandwich. Repeat with remaining pieces.

❺ Continue with steps (3), (4), (5) and (6) on page 94.

STUFFED JALAPEÑO PEPPERS

Substitute: *8 - 12 Jalapeño peppers* for the *tofu*

❶ Cut each pepper in half lengthwise. Remove and discard seeds and membrane.

❷ Fill pepper halves with 1½ - 2 teaspoons stuffing.

❸ Continue with steps (3), (4), (5) and (6) on page 94.

STUFFED BITTER MELONS

Substitute: *1 - 3 Bitter melons* for the *tofu*

❶ Cut bitter melons, crosswise, into about ½- to 1-inch sections.

❷ Scoop out and discard seeds.

❸ Fill bitter melon sections with 2 - 3 teaspoons stuffing. Leveling and smoothing out both ends.

❹ Continue with steps (3), (4), (5) and (6) on page 94.

STUFFED CUCUMBER

Substitute: *1 - 2 Cucumbers* for the *tofu*

❶ Cut cucumber, crosswise, into ¾- to 1½-inch sections.

❷ Scoop out and discard seeds.

❸ Fill cucumber sections with 3 - 4 teaspoons stuffing. Leveling and smoothing out both ends.

❹ Continue with steps (3), (4), (5) and (6) on page 94.

MA PO TOFU

serves 3 - 6

¼ pound ground pork	)
2 teaspoons regular soy sauce	) Combine. Mix well. Can be done
1 tablespoon ginger wine, p. 16	) the day before and refrigerated.
½ teaspoon sugar	)

½ - 2 teaspoons Asian chili sauce
1 - 2 cloves garlic Minced
1 pound firm or extra firm tofu Cut into about ½-inch cubes
1 tablespoon bean sauce
2 scallions, white part Minced
½ teaspoon salt or to taste
¼ cup chicken broth or as needed
2 tablespoons oil
1 teaspoon sesame oil (optional)

2 teaspoons cornstarch	) Combine in a small bowl.
1 tablespoon water	) Stir well just before adding to wok.

(1) Heat wok. Add oil. Swirl to coat wok. Add chili sauce and garlic. Stir-fry over high heat 10 seconds. Add pork. Stir-fry until color changes, about 2 minutes.

(2) Stir in tofu, bean sauce, scallions, salt and broth. Bring to boil. Simmer 2 minutes.

(3) Thicken with cornstarch mixture. Stir in sesame oil. Serve hot.

****

Practical Variation

MA PO TOFU WITH MISO

Substitute: *¼ pound ground beef* for the *ground pork*
           1½ - 2 tablespoons miso for the *bean sauce*
Add: *2 - 3 tablespoons green peas* during step (2)

VEGETABLES

98
Asparagus Salad
Asparagus Salad with Walnut Oil
Bean Sprouts Salad
Green Bean Salad

99
Asparagus in Garlic Oil
Curried Asparagus in Garlic Oil
Chinese Long Beans in Garlic Oil

100
Sesame Broccoli Florets
Broccoli in Brown Sauce
Sesame Broccoli Rabe
Sesame Choy Sum

101
Steamed Broccoli
Steamed Gai Lan
Steamed Broccoli Florets & Cauliflower
Steamed Ginger, Sesame Broccoli

102
Stir-fry Cabbage
Spicy Cabbage
Spicy Napa Cabbage
Stir-fry Bok Choy

103
Hot & Sour Napa Cabbage
Hot & Sour Green Cabbage

104
Spicy Eggplant
Spicy Green Soy Beans
Spicy Summer Squash

105
Braised Kohlrabi
Braised Angled Luffa
Braised Chinese Radish
Braised Jerusalem Artichoke
Braised Fuzzy Melon

106
Sesame Lettuce

106
Lettuce with Oyster Sauce

107
Heart of Napa with Cream Sauce
Savoy Cabbage with Cream Sauce
Heart of Bok Choy with Cream Sauce
Shanghai Bok Choy with Cream Sauce

108
Braised Red Radishes with Dried Scallops
Braised Chinese Radish with Dried Scallops
Braised Turnip with Dried Scallops
Braised Fuzzy Melon with Dried Scallops
Braised Chayote with Dried Scallops

109
Tri-color Stir-fry

109
Stir-fry Brussels Sprouts

110
Swiss Chard with Fermented Bean Curd
Ong Choi with Fermented Bean Curd
Spinach with Fermented Bean Curd

ASPARAGUS SALAD

serves 4 - 6

1 - 1½ pounds fresh asparagus Peeled, p. 99. Remove scales, p. 99. Washed. Roll cut.

1 - 2 cloves garlic Crushed	) Combine.
1 tablespoon regular soy sauce	) This is the dressing.
1 tablespoon Asian sesame oil	) Can be done the day before.
2 teaspoons finely crushed Chinese	) Discard garlic before tossing
rock sugar or *white sugar*	) with asparagus.

1 tablespoon toasted sesame seeds

(1) Bring a large pot of water to boil. Drop in asparagus. Remove pot from heat. Let asparagus blanch for 1 minute.

(2) Drain asparagus. Cool thoroughly under cold running water. Drain and pat dry thoroughly with paper towel or clean kitchen towel. Can be done the day before and refrigerated.

(3) Toss cooled asparagus with dressing. Marinate ½ hour before serving but not more than 1 hour.

(4) Arrange asparagus on serving dish. Garnish with sesame seeds. Serve.

****

Practical Variations

ASPARAGUS SALAD WITH WALNUT OIL

Substitute: *1 tablespoon walnut oil* for the *Asian sesame oil*
1 tablespoon roasted walnuts for the *sesame seeds* Coarsely chop walnuts.

BEAN SPROUTS SALAD

Substitute: *1 pound bean sprouts* for the *asparagus* Blanch bean sprouts for 10 seconds.

GREEN BEAN SALAD

Substitute: *1 pound green beans* for the *asparagus* Simmer green beans for 2 - 3 minutes or until crisp tender.

Add: *¼ - 1 teaspoon Asian chili sauce* to the dressing

ASPARAGUS IN GARLIC OIL
serves 4 - 6

1 pound fresh asparagus Peeled. Remove scales. Washed. Roll cut.
1 - 2 tablespoons vegetable oil
1 - 6 cloves garlic Crushed
2 - 3 slices fresh ginger
¼ teaspoon kosher salt or to taste

(1) Heat wok. Add oil. Swirl to coat wok. Add garlic. Let garlic and ginger simmer in oil over medium heat until they begin to brown lightly. Remove and discard garlic and ginger, if desired.

(2) Add salt and asparagus. Stir-fry over high heat until asparagus changes to a bright green color and a shade under desired doneness. Remove to a serving platter and serve. (Asparagus will continue to cook in its own heat and will be just the way you like it when it reaches the table.)

Peeling asparagus: With a sharp paring knife, start peeling at the root end to about ¼ - ½ the length of the spear. A vegetable peeler works well also.

Scaling asparagus: Remove a few scales, if there is no sand under the scales, then there is no need to remove any more. If there is sand, scales on the whole batch will need to be removed.

****

Practical Variations

CURRIED ASPARAGUS IN GARLIC OIL

Add: *½ - 1 teaspoon curry powder* the same time as asparagus.
           1 tablespoon lemon juice Stir in lemon juice just before removing to serving platter.

CHINESE LONG BEANS IN GARLIC OIL

Substitute: *1 pound green skin Chinese long beans* for the *asparagus* Remove ends from beans. Cut into 1 - 2-inch lengths.

Add: *2 - 4 tablespoons broth or water* Add to wok 1 tablespoon at a time during step (2) if wok is dry.

SESAME BROCCOLI FLORETS

serves 4 - 6

1 bunch fresh broccoli Cut florets into bite-size pieces. Blanch. (Save stems for Tri-color Stir-fry on page 109)
1 - 2 tablespoons oil
½ teaspoon kosher salt or to taste
1 - 3 cloves garlic Finely minced
1 tablespoon Asian sesame oil or to taste
1 - 2 tablespoons broth or *water*, if needed
1 tablespoon toasted sesame seeds

(1) Heat wok. Add oil. Swirl to coat wok. Add salt and garlic. Stir-fry 30 seconds over medium-high heat. Add broccoli. Stir-fry over high heat until reached desired doneness, about 2 minutes. Adding broth or water if wok is dry.
(2) Stir in sesame oil. Remove to serving platter. Garnish with sesame seeds. Serve hot or at room temperature.

Blanching Broccoli: Bring a large pot of water to boil. Remove from heat. Plunge broccoli into boiling water. Stir and drain immediately. Cool broccoli under cold running water. Drain.

Practical Variations

BROCCOLI IN BROWN SAUCE

Substitute: *1 - 2 tablespoons oyster sauce* for the *salt*
Add: *¼ - 1 teaspoon Asian chili sauce or to taste*
Add oyster sauce and chili sauce to wok at the same time as broccoli.

SESAME BROCCOLI RABE

Substitute: *1 pound broccoli rabe* for the *broccoli* Cut into 1½-inch lengths.
Add: *½ - 1 teaspoon sugar* Add to wok the same time as broccoli rabe.

SESAME CHOY SUM

Substitute: *1 pound choy sum* for the *broccoli* Cut into 1½-inch lengths
1 - 2 tablespoons oyster sauce for the *salt* Add to wok the same time as the choy sum.

STEAMED BROCCOLI

serves 4 - 6

1 bunch fresh broccoli Cut florets into bite-size pieces. Peel stems. Cut into
    bite-size pieces. Blanch, p. 100, (optional)

2 - 3 slices cooked ham (optional) Cut into thin strips.

1 - 2 tablespoons toasted pine nuts

oil or *melted butter* (optional)

kosher salt to taste

***

(1) Bring water in steamer base to boil.

(2) Line steamer basket or steamer rack with a layer of cheesecloth. Spread
    blanched broccoli on top. Cover. Steam over high heat until reached desired
    doneness, about 2 - 2½ minutes.

(3) Remove steamed broccoli to a serving platter. Toss with oil or butter and salt
    if desired. Arrange ham on top. Garnish with pine nuts. Serve.

****

Practical Variations

STEAMED GAI LAN

Substitute: *1½ pounds gai lan* for the *broccoli* Leave gai lan whole. Split
               thicker stalks to make all the stalks uniform. Arrange steamed gai lan
               lengthwise on serving platter. Using kitchen scissors, cut into 2 - 4
               sections.

STEAMED BROCCOLI FLORETS & CAULIFLOWER

Substitute: *¾ pound broccoli florets* for the *bunch of broccoli* Cut into
               bite-size pieces.

Add: *¾ pound cauliflower* Cut into bite-size pieces.

STEAMED GINGER, SESAME BROCCOLI

Substitute: *1 teaspoon sesame oil* for the *oil* or *melted butter*
               1 tablespoon toasted sesame seeds for the *pine nuts*

Add: *1 teaspoon shredded ginger* Toss with sesame oil and salt during
               step (3).

My Students' Favorite Chinese Recipes, updated edition   Vegetables **101**

STIR-FRY CABBAGE

1 pound green or *savoy cabbage* Cut into about ½-inch wide strips or bite-size chunks.

1 - 2 tablespoons oil

1 teaspoon kosher salt or to taste

¼ - 1 teaspoon Asian sesame oil (optional)

2 - 4 tablespoons water or broth

(1) Heat wok. Add oil. Swirl to coat wok. Add salt and cabbage. Stir-fry over high to medium-high heat for 1 minute.

(2) Add water or broth 1 tablespoon at a time if wok seems dry. Continue stir-frying until cabbage reaches desired doneness.

(3) Stir in sesame oil, if using. Remove to serving platter. Serve hot or at room temperature.

NOTE: This is **a fast and easy dish**. Just what a in-a-hurry cook needs.

KITCHEN HINT: Elevate this dish by garnishing with edible flowers, tossing in some chopped red, yellow and/or green peppers or tossing in some grated or shredded carrots.

****

Practical Variations

SPICY CABBAGE

Eliminate: *salt*

Add: *1 - 2 cloves garlic* Minced. Brown lightly before adding cabbage.

          ¼ - 1 teaspoon Asian Chili sauce or to taste Add to wok same time as cabbage.

          ½ teaspoon brown sugar (optional) Add to wok during step (2)

          1 - 2 tablespoons regular soy sauce Add to wok during step (2)

SPICY NAPA CABBAGE

Substitute: *1 pound napa cabbage* for the *green* or *savoy cabbage*

          1 - 2 tablespoons oyster sauce for the *regular soy sauce* Add to wok during step (2)

Add: *ground white* or *black pepper to taste* Add same time as cabbage

          Asian chili sauce to taste Add same time as cabbage

STIR-FRY BOK CHOY

Substitute: *1 pound bok choy* for the *cabbage*

HOT & SOUR NAPA CABBAGE

serves 4 - 6

1 pound napa cabbage Cut lengthwise into about ½-inch wide and 2-inch long strips.

1 - 2 tablespoons oil

3 - 5 dried whole chili peppers or to taste

1 tablespoon brown sugar

1 - 2 tablespoons regular soy sauce

1 - 2 tablespoons Chinkiang vinegar

1 teaspoon Asian sesame oil

½ teaspoon kosher salt or to taste

¼ - 1 teaspoon Asian sesame oil (optional)

1 tablespoon toasted black or *white sesame seeds*

(1) Heat wok. Add oil. Swirl to coat wok. Add whole chili peppers to hot oil.

(2) Add napa cabbage to wok as soon as chili peppers turn black. Stir-fry over high to medium-high heat until cabbage begins to wilt.

(3) Add sugar, soy sauce and salt. Continue stir-frying until cabbage loses its raw taste but is still crunchy.

(4) Stir in Chinkiang vinegar and sesame oil. Remove to serving platter. Garnish with sesame seeds. Serve hot or at room temperature.

KITCHEN HINT: When toasting black sesame seeds, add a few white ones. When the white sesame seeds are toasted, you know the black ones will be toasted also.

KITCHEN HINT: Substitute balsamic vinegar for the Chinkiang vinegar. Cider vinegar will work for this recipe also.

****

Practical Variations

HOT & SOUR GREEN CABBAGE

Substitute: *1 pound green cabbage* for the *napa cabbage* Cut green cabbage into ½-inch strips or chunks.

Add: *1 - 2 cloves garlic* Minced. Add to wok same time as chili peppers.

¼ cup carrot slices Add to wok same time as cabbage.

SPICY EGGPLANT

serves 4 - 6

¾ pound Chinese eggplant Remove and discard cap. Cut eggplant, crosswise, into 2-inch pieces. Cut each piece, lengthwise, into 4 or 6 logs.

2 tablespoons vegetable oil

2 cloves garlic Minced

¼ - 1 teaspoon Asian chili sauce or to taste

1 tablespoon ginger wine, p. 16

2 tablespoons regular soy sauce

1 teaspoon sugar

¼ - ½ cup chicken broth or *vegetable broth*

1 tablespoon Chinkiang vinegar

2 teaspoons Asian sesame oil

1 scallion Cleaned. Sliced thinly

1 tablespoon toasted white sesame seeds

(1) Heat wok. Add 2 tablespoons vegetable oil. Swirl to coat wok. Add garlic and chili sauce. Stir-fry over medium high heat for 30 seconds. Add eggplant. Stir-fry over medium heat until soft, adding broth 1 tablespoon at a time if wok seems dry.

(2) Add ginger wine, soy sauce and sugar. Stir-fry about 1 minute. Add broth. Bring to a boil. Cover and cook until just about all the liquid is absorbed.

(3) Stir in Chinkiang vinegar and sesame oil. Remove to serving platter. Garnish with scallion and sesame seeds. Serve hot or cold.

****

Practical Variations

SPICY GREEN SOY BEANS

Substitute: *½ - ¾ pound shelled frozen green soy beans* for the *eggplant*

Add: *½ - ¾ pound potatoes* Peel. Cut into about ¼-inch cubes. Add to wok at the same time as soy beans.

SPICY SUMMER SQUASH

Substitute: *¾ - 1 pound zucchini* for the *eggplant*

Add: *1 small onion* Thinly sliced. Add to wok at the same time as garlic.

Braised Kohlrabi

serves 3 - 6

4 kohlrabi (1 - 1½ pounds) Peel. Cut into about ½-inch chunks.

2 - 3 carrots Peeled. Cut into ½-inch thick slices.

1 15-ounce can peeled or *unpeeled straw mushrooms* Rinsed. Drained.

¼ teaspoon salt or to taste

¾ cup chicken broth or *vegetable broth*

2 teaspoons cornstarch) Combine in a small bowl.
1 tablespoon water) Stir well just before adding to saucepan.

(1) In a saucepan, combine kohlrabi, carrots, salt and broth. Bring to a boil. Cover and simmer 10 minutes.

(2) Add straw mushrooms. Simmer another 5 minutes or until vegetables reach desired doneness. Up to this point can be done ahead of time.

(3) Thicken with cornstarch mixture. Serve hot.

****

Practical Variations

Braised Angled Luffa

Substitute: *1 pound angled luffa* for the *kohlrabi* Remove and discard ridges. Peeled (leave some of the skin on for texture). Add during step (2).

Braised Chinese Radish

Substitute: *1 pound Chinese radish* for the *kohlrabi* Peeled. Cut into about ½-inch chunks.

Braised Jerusalem Artichoke

Substitute: *1 pound Jerusalem artichoke* for the *kohlrabi* Peeled. Cut into about ½-inch chunks.

Braised Fuzzy Melon

Substitute: *1 pound fuzzy melon* for the *kohlrabi* Peeled. Cut into about ½-inch chunks.

SESAME LETTUCE

serves 3 - 6

1 head iceberg lettuce Washed. Drained. Break into large pieces.
1 - 2 tablespoons vegetable oil
2 slices ginger
1 teaspoon kosher salt or to taste
2 teaspoons sesame oil or to taste
1 - 2 tablespoons toasted sesame seeds

(1) Heat wok. Add vegetable oil. Swirl to coat wok. Add ginger. Stir-fry over high heat 30 seconds. Add salt and lettuce. Stir-fry until lettuce is wilted and just heated through, about 2 minutes. Stir in sesame oil. Remove and discard ginger.

(2) Remove lettuce to serving platter, draining off excess liquid. Garnish with sesame seeds.

****

LETTUCE WITH OYSTER SAUCE

serves 3 - 6

1 head Romaine lettuce Washed. Drained. Break each leaf into 2 or 3 pieces.
1 - 2 tablespoons vegetable oil
1 clove garlic Crushed
2 slices ginger
¼ teaspoon kosher salt or to taste
ground white or *black pepper to taste*
1 - 2 tablespoons oyster sauce or to taste

(1) Heat wok. Add oil. Swirl to coat wok. Add garlic and ginger. Stir-fry over medium-high heat until garlic begins to brown. Remove and discard garlic and ginger.

(2) Add salt and lettuce. Stir-fry until lettuce is wilted and just heated through, about 2 minutes. Drain off excess liquid, if any.

(3) Stir in white or black pepper and oyster sauce. Remove lettuce to serving platter. Serve.

NOTE: These 2 recipes are great for using the mature and less tender lettuce leaves.

HEART OF NAPA WITH CREAM SAUCE serves 4 - 6

1 ½ pounds napa cabbage heart Separate leaves. Cut leaves into 3 or 4
   lengthwise strips. Cut strips into 2-inch lengths.

½ teaspoon kosher salt or to taste

½ teaspoon sugar or to taste

1 - 2 tablespoons oil

½ cup chicken broth or *vegetable broth*

3 tablespoons heavy cream

½ - 1 slice cooked ham (optional) Thinly shredded.

1 tablespoon cornstarch	) Combine in a small bowl.
2 tablespoons broth or water	) Stir well just before adding to wok.

(1) Heat wok. Add oil. Swirl to coat wok. Add salt and napa. Stir-fry over high to
   medium-high heat until napa is tender, adding broth 1 tablespoon at a time
   if wok seems dry.

(2) Stir in sugar and remaining broth. Bring to a boil. Thicken with cornstarch
   mixture. Stir in cream. Remove to serving platter. Garnish with ham. Serve.

****

Practical Variations

SAVOY CABBAGE WITH CREAM SAUCE

Substitute: *1 pound savoy cabbage* for the *napa cabbage* Cut into about
   ¼-inch wide long strips

Add: *1 tablespoon toasted pine nuts* Sprinkle nuts on top of ham.

HEART OF BOK CHOY WITH CREAM SAUCE

Substitute: *1 ½ pounds bok choy heart* for the *napa cabbage* Slant cut into
   about ½-inch wide strips.

SHANGHAI BOK CHOY WITH CREAM SAUCE

Substitute: *1 pound Shanghai bok choy* for the *napa cabbage* Cut into
   about 1-inch lengths.

Add: *1 tablespoon toasted sliced almonds* Sprinkle almonds on top of
   ham.

BRAISED RED RADISHES WITH DRIED SCALLOPS serves 4 - 6

1 pound large red radishes Peeled

3 - 4 dried scallops (optional) Rinsed. Cover with water and soak at least 1 hour to soften. Gently rub soaked scallops with fingers to separate the fibers.

1 tablespoon ginger wine, p. 16

2 slices ginger from ginger wine

½ cup chicken broth or *vegetable broth*

kosher salt to taste

1 scallion Cleaned. Sliced thinly.

2 teaspoons cornstarch	) Combine in a small bowl.
1 tablespoon water	) Stir well just before adding to saucepan.

(1) In a saucepan, combine radishes, scallops, water from soaking scallops, ginger wine, ginger and broth. Bring to a boil. Cover. Simmer about 30 minutes or until radishes are soft. Up to this point can be done ahead of time.

(2) Thicken with cornstarch mixture. Add salt to taste. Stir in scallion. Serve hot.

****

Practical Variations

BRAISED CHINESE RADISH WITH DRIED SCALLOPS

Substitute: *1 pound Chinese radish* for the *red radishes* Peel radish. Cut into about 1-inch chunks.

BRAISED TURNIP WITH DRIED SCALLOPS

Substitute: *1 pound turnips* for the *red radishes* Peel turnips. Cut into about 1-inch chunks.

BRAISED FUZZY MELON WITH DRIED SCALLOPS

Substitute: *1 pound fuzzy melon* for the *red radishes* Peel fuzzy melon. Cut into about 1-inch chunks.

BRAISED CHAYOTE WITH DRIED SCALLOPS

Substitute: *2 - 3 chayotes (about 1 pound)* for the *red radishes* Peel chayotes. Cut in half lengthwise. Remove and discard seed. Cut into about 1-inch chunks.

TRI-COLOR STIR-FRY

serves 4 - 6

1 - 2 carrots Peeled. Cut into about ⅛-inch thick circles.
1 8-ounce can sliced water chestnuts Drained
3 - 4 broccoli main stems Peeled. Cut into about ¼-inch thick circles.
1 - 2 tablespoons oil
½ teaspoon kosher salt or to taste
2 - 4 tablespoons water or broth

(1) Heat wok. Add oil. Swirl to coat wok. Add salt, carrots, water chestnuts and broccoli stems. Stir-fry over high to medium-high heat until vegetables reach desired doneness, adding water or broth 1 tablespoon at a time if wok seems dry.

(2) Remove to serving platter. Serve hot or at room temperature.

****

STIR-FRY BRUSSELS SPROUTS

serves 4 - 6

¾ pound Brussels sprouts Trim off mature leaves. Washed. Drained. Cut small Brussels sprouts in halves; large ones into quarters.
1 carrot Peeled. Cut into about ¼-inch thick circles.
¾ teaspoon kosher salt or to taste
¼ teaspoon sugar
3 slices fresh ginger
2 cloves garlic Crushed
2 tablespoons oil
1 - 2 tablespoons broth or *water* if needed

(1) Heat wok. Add oil. Swirl to coat wok. Add ginger and garlic. Stir-fry over high heat 30 seconds or until garlic begins to brown. Remove and discard ginger and garlic.

(2) Add salt, Brussels sprouts and carrot. Mix well. Sprinkle on sugar. Stir-fry until Brussels sprouts reach desired doneness, about 3 minutes, adding broth or water 1 tablespoon at a time if wok seems dry. Serve hot.

SWISS CHARD WITH FERMENTED BEAN CURD

serves 4 - 6

1 - 1½ pounds Swiss chard Washed. Cut into bite-size pieces, keep stems and leaves separate.

1 - 2 cloves garlic Minced

2 slices ginger from ginger wine, p. 16

1 cube fermented bean curd Crushed

½ teaspoon kosher salt or to taste

1 - 2 tablespoons oil

(1) Heat wok. Add oil. Add garlic and ginger. Stir-fry until garlic is translucent. Add fermented bean curd.
(2) Add Swiss chard stems. Stir-fry about 2 minutes or until partially cooked.
(3) Add Swiss chard leaves. Stir-fry until stem and leaves reach desired doneness. Add salt to taste. Serve hot.

****

Practical Variations

ONG CHOI WITH FERMENTED BEAN CURD

Substitute: *1 - 1½ pounds ong choi* for the *Swiss chard* Wash ong choi thoroughly. Break, at stem, into shorter lengths. Do not separate leaves from stems.

SPINACH WITH FERMENTED BEAN CURD

Substitute: *1 - 1½ pounds spinach* for the *Swiss chard* Wash spinach thoroughly. Cut into shorter lengths if desired. Use both leaves and stems.

CHICKEN, DUCK & TURKEY

112
Minced Duck with Pine Nuts
Minced Chicken with Peanuts in Steamed Pita Pockets
Minced Pork with Almonds Tortilla Rolls
Frozen Tofu with Pine Nuts

114
5-Spice Oven Fried Chicken
South of the Border Oven Fried Chicken

115
Moo Goo Gai Pan
(Chicken with Fresh Mushrooms)

116
Lemon Chicken
Lemon Tofu
Oven-fried Sesame Lemon Chicken
Low-fat Lemon Chicken

118
Sa Bo Chicken

120
Sesame Pineapple Chicken
Mushroom & Chinese Sausage Chicken
Prosciutto & Scallion Chicken

122
Braised Chayote Chicken
Braised Chicken with Chinese Radish

123
Chicken, Snow Peas & Baby Corn
Chicken with Broccoli

124
Chicken in Hoisin Sauce
Chicken & Tofu in Hoisin Sauce
Tofu in Hoisin Sauce

125
Curry Chicken
Curry Lamb Shank

126
Steamed Chicken

MINCED DUCK WITH PINE NUTS

serves 3 - 6

1 pound boneless & skinless duck meat Cut into about ¼-inch cubes or
   coarsely minced.

½ teaspoon kosher salt or to taste)	
½ teaspoon sugar	) Combine.
1 tablespoon ginger wine, p. 16	) Add duck. Mix well.
1 tablespoon regular soy sauce	) Marinate ½ hour if time allows.
dash of white pepper or to taste	) Can be done the day before and
1 teaspoon cornstarch	) refrigerated.
1 egg yolk	)

6 - 8 Chinese dried mushrooms (about 1-inch in diameter) Soak in water for
   ½ hour or more to soften. Squeeze out excess water. Remove and discard
   stems. Cut caps into about ¼-inch cubes.

1 8-ounce can bamboo shoot tips or *chunks* Cut into about ¼-inch cubes.

1 red onion (about 6 ounces) Peel. Cut into about ¼-inch cubes.

¾ cup ¼-inch (about) cubes green pepper

4 slices fresh ginger from ginger wine, p. 16

¼ - 1 teaspoon Asian chili sauce (optional)

4 ounces toasted pine nuts

1 teaspoon kosher salt or to taste

3 - 4 tablespoons oil

1 - 2 teaspoons sesame oil or to taste

1½ teaspoons cornstarch	) Combine in a small bowl.
2 tablespoons water or broth	) Stir well just before adding to wok.

1 - 2 heads Boston or Romaine lettuce Separate leaves. Wash and pat dry
   well. Arrange on a serving platter.

hoisin sauce Place in a small serving dish.

2 - 4 tablespoons chicken broth or as needed

(1) Heat wok. Add 2 - 3 tablespoons oil. Swirl to coat wok. Add ginger and chili
   sauce. Stir-fry over medium-high heat for 10 seconds. Add duck. Stir-fry
   over high heat until color changes, adding broth 1 tablespoon at a time if wok
   is dry. Remove to a plate. Remove and discard ginger slices.

(2) Add 1 tablespoon oil to wok or frying pan, if needed. Add salt, mushrooms,
   bamboo shoots and onion. Stir-fry over medium-high or high heat for about

MINCED DUCK WITH PINE NUTS (continued)

2 minutes or until mushrooms are fragrant, adding broth 1 tablespoon at a time if wok is dry.

(3) Add green pepper and duck. Stir-fry until duck is cooked, about 5 minutes. Thicken with cornstarch mixture. Add sesame oil. Mix well. Remove to serving platter. Sprinkle pine nuts on top. Garnish with a few lettuce leaves.

To serve: Brush a little hoisin sauce on a lettuce leaf. Spoon some hot duck mixture on top. Fold and eat with fingers.

****

Practical Variations

MINCED CHICKEN WITH PEANUTS IN STEAMED PITA POCKETS

Substitute: *1 pound coarsely ground chicken* for the *duck*
2 - 4 ounces toasted, unsalted peanuts for the *pine nuts* Chop peanuts coarsely (optional).

Add: *Small pita bread* Cut in halves. Steam, p. 149.

To serve: Brush a bit of hoisin sauce on the inside of steamed pita. Tuck in a lettuce leaf. Fill with hot chicken mixture. Serve.

MINCED PORK WITH ALMONDS TORTILLA ROLLS

Substitute: *1 pound of coarsely ground pork* for the *duck*
2 - 4 ounces toasted, slivered almonds for the *pine nuts*

Add: *Small flour tortilla* Steam (same as steam pita, p. 149 but leave tortilla whole) **or** Wrap tortilla in foil. Place in a 300° oven for 10 minutes to soften.

To serve: Brush a bit of hoisin sauce on one side of steamed tortilla. Line with 1 or 2 lettuce leaves, spoon on some pork mixture, roll and enjoy.

FROZEN TOFU WITH PINE NUTS

Substitute: *1 pound frozen tofu*, p. 73, for the *duck* Thaw tofu. Squeeze out excess water. Cut into ¼ inch cubes or coarsely crumbled.
1 tablespoon mushroom soy sauce for the *regular soy sauce*
1 whole egg for the *egg yolk*

5-SPICE OVEN FRIED CHICKEN   serves 6 - 8

4 - 5 pounds chicken legs Rinsed and pat dry. Separate thighs and
drumsticks.

1 tablespoon kosher salt	)
1 teaspoon sugar or *honey*	) Combine. This is the marinade.
2 tablespoons ginger wine, p. 16	) Add chicken. Mix well.
2 teaspoons 5-spice powder	) Marinate 2 hours or overnight
2 teaspoons mushroom soy sauce	) in the refrigerator.
1 teaspoon regular soy sauce	)

2 cups crushed cornflakes (about)	) Combine in a plastic bag or on
¼ cup sesame seeds (optional)	) a plate.

1 - 2 whole eggs Crack into a deep plate or a mixing bowl. Beat lightly to
combine yolk and white.

¼ - ½ cup vegetable oil

(1) Position an oven rack in middle of oven. Preheat oven to 425°.
(2) Dip chicken legs in beaten eggs. Roll in cornflakes mixture to coat well.
Place on rimmed baking sheet or a shallow baking pan. Dribble oil over
coated chicken.
(3) Bake, in middle of oven, uncovered, at 425° for 35 minutes.

KITCHEN HINT: Chili lovers: Add *¼ - 2 teaspoons Asian chili sauce* to the marinade.
Mushroom soy sauce unavailable? Substitute *dark soy sauce* or *regular soy
sauce*.

****

Practical Variation

SOUTH OF THE BORDER OVEN FRIED CHICKEN

Substitute: *1 - 5 finely minced jalapeño peppers* for the *5-spice powder*
¼ cup finely chopped pecans, walnuts or *almonds* for the
sesame seeds

Add: *¼ cup finely chopped cilantro* to *cornflakes mixture*

MOO GOO GAI PAN (CHICKEN WITH FRESH MUSHROOMS) serves 3 - 5

1 pound boneless & skinless chicken breast Cut into about ¼-inch thick
  slices.

1 teaspoon kosher salt or to taste	) Combine.
1 teaspoon sugar	) Stir in chicken. Marinate ½
1 tablespoon ginger wine, p. 16	) hour if time permits.
1 tablespoon regular soy sauce	) Can be done the day before
dash of white pepper or to taste	) and refrigerated.

½ - 1 pound fresh mushrooms Cut in about ½-inch thick slices.
1 small onion Peeled. Cut into 6 or 8 lengthwise sections.
½ - 1 green pepper Cut into strips.
½ - 1 red pepper Cut into strips.
1 dried chili pepper (optional) Discard seeds. Thinly slice pod.
½ teaspoon kosher salt or to taste
3 tablespoons oil
¼ - ½ cup chicken broth

1½ teaspoons cornstarch	) Combine in a small bowl.
2 tablespoons water or broth	) Stir well just before adding to wok.

(1) Heat wok. Add 1 tablespoon oil. Swirl to coat wok. Add salt, mushrooms and
    onion. Stir-fry over medium-high heat for 2 minutes. Add green and red
    pepper. Stir-fry over high heat about 1 minute, adding broth 1 tablespoon at
    a time if wok is dry. Remove vegetables and any liquid to a plate.

(2) Add remaining oil to wok. Heat until smoking. Add chili pepper, stir-fry 10
    seconds. Add chicken. Stir-fry over high heat until chicken changes color,
    adding broth 1 tablespoon at a time if wok is dry. Return vegetables and any
    liquid to wok. Stir-fry until chicken is thoroughly cooked.

(3) Add additional broth, as needed for gravy. Bring to a boil. Thicken with corn-
    starch mixture. Mix well. Serve hot.

KITCHEN HINT: For a darker chicken color, substitute *dark soy sauce* or *mushroom soy
        sauce* for part or all of the *regular soy sauce*.
        Fresh chili pepper or *Asian chili sauce* can be substituted for the *dried
        chili pepper*.

LEMON CHICKEN

serves 3 - 5

1 pound boneless & skinless chicken breast halves Rinsed and pat dry
   Flatten each with a mallet to even thickness.

½ teaspoon kosher salt	) Combine.
½ teaspoon sugar	) This is the marinade.
¼ teaspoon white pepper or to taste	) Add chicken. Coat well.
1 tablespoon ginger wine, p. 16	) Marinate ½ hour but no
2 tablespoons fresh lemon juice	) more than 2 hours.

¼ cup flour	) Combine on a plate or in a clean plastic bag.
¼ cup cornstarch	) This is coating for the chicken.

2 tablespoons sugar	)
1 tablespoon cornstarch	)
1 tablespoon regular soy sauce	) Combine in a small saucepan.
3 tablespoons catsup	) This is the lemon sauce.
2 tablespoons fresh lemon juice	)
½ cup water	)

2 or more cups shredded lettuce
oil for deep frying

(1) Heat oil, in a wok or frying pan, to 375°. Coat marinated chicken breast with
     flour and cornstarch mixture. Deep fry until lightly browned and chicken is
     thoroughly cooked. Remove and drain on paper towel.

(2) Line serving platter with shredded lettuce. Slice fried chicken and arrange
     on bed of lettuce.

(3) Bring lemon sauce to a boil, stirring constantly. Spoon over sliced chicken.
     Serve at once.

****

Practical Variations

LEMON TOFU

Substitute: ***1 pound extra-firm tofu*** for the ***chicken*** Cut drained tofu into
     about ¼-inch thick slices. Pat dry.

OVEN-FRIED SESAME LEMON CHICKEN

Add: **1 teaspoon Asian sesame oil** to the marinade

Substitute: **1 cup crushed crispy rice** and **2 tablespoons black or white sesame seeds** for the **flour** and **cornstarch**

Have ready: **1 - 2 eggs** Lightly beaten

               2 - 3 tablespoons oil

Cooking: ❶ Preheat oven to 425°.

            ❷ Coat marinated chicken with beaten egg.

            ❸ Roll in crispy rice and sesame seed mixture. Place on rimmed baking sheet or shallow baking pan. Dribble with oil.

            ❹ Bake 9 - 12 minutes or until chicken is thoroughly cooked.

            ❺ Line serving platter with shredded lettuce. Slice cooked chicken and arrange on bed of lettuce.

            ❻ Bring lemon sauce to a boil, stirring constantly. Spoon over sliced chicken. Serve at once.

LOW-FAT LEMON CHICKEN

Eliminate: **¼ cup flour** and **¼ cup cornstarch**.

Cooking: ❶ Cut chicken (do not flatten) into about ¼-inch thick slices. Add to marinade.

            ❷ In a large frying pan, bring lemon sauce to a boil, stirring constantly.

            ❸ Add marinated chicken. Mix well. Bring to a boil. Lower heat to medium-low. Cook chicken, covered, for 5 - 8 minutes, or until chicken is completely cooked, stirring occasionally.

            ❹ Ladle onto lettuce lined serving platter. Serve hot.

KITCHEN HINT: This version tastes better the next day. **Great do-ahead dish.**

SA BO CHICKEN

serves 5 - 8

8 chicken thighs *(about 2½ pounds)* Washed and pat dry. Remove and discard skin. Cut through bones into bite-size pieces.

1 teaspoon kosher salt or to taste	) Combine. Add chicken and
1 teaspoon crushed Chinese rock	) mix well. Marinate ½ hour if
sugar or **honey**	) time permits.
2 tablespoons ginger wine, p. 16	) Can be done the day before
2 tablespoons mushroom soy sauce	) and refrigerated.

8 - 10 dried Chinese mushrooms Soak in water for at least ½ hour to soften. Squeeze out excess water. Remove and discard stems. Coarsely chop caps.

12 dried tiger lily flowers Soak in water for at least ½ hour to soften. Remove and discard any woody parts. Coarsely chop flowers.

4 cloves garlic Thinly sliced.

2 scallions Thinly sliced.

1 - 2 tablespoons oil

1 teaspoon cornstarch	) Combine in a small bowl.
2 tablespoons water or **broth**	) Stir well just before adding to wok.

(1) Heat wok. Add oil. Swirl to coat wok. Add garlic and scallions. Stir-fry over medium-high heat until fragrant. Add mushrooms and tiger lily flowers. Stir-fry over medium-high heat for another 2 minutes.

(2) Drain chicken (reserve marinade). Add drained chicken to wok. Stir-fry over high heat until chicken looks glazed. Add reserved marinade. Stir-fry until liquid is absorbed. Stir in cornstarch mixture.

(3) Transfer chicken to sa bo, p. 119. Cover. Place in middle of cold oven. Turn oven to 350°. Bake 30 minutes. Turn off oven. Let stand in hot oven 15 minutes. Serve hot.

KITCHEN HINT: **Dark soy sauce** may be substituted for the **mushroom soy sauce.**
KITCHEN HINT: Substitute an oven proof covered casserole for the sa bo.

NOTE: Cutting through the bones may result in some small bone chips in the finished dish. If this is a problem, use 2 pounds boneless chicken thighs instead.

SA BO CHICKEN (continued)

The drawings below are all purpose SA BO (Chinese sandpot). They are used to cook rice, make stews, simmer soups but not for stir-frying.

These all purpose sa bos are available in various sizes, with or without protective wire, with a long handle and a loop or just 2 loops. The inside has a dark brown glaze, while the outside is left unglazed. The cover is unglazed on the inside and glazed on the outside and has a small steam hole near the rim. A 3-quart size is probably the best size for most household use.

Food cooks faster in a sa bo and less liquid is needed. Use about ¼ - ½ less liquid than you would in a stainless steel pot. See page 36 for more information on the use and care of sa bo.

An oven-proof covered casserole or an oven-proof pot may be used as substitute for sa bo.

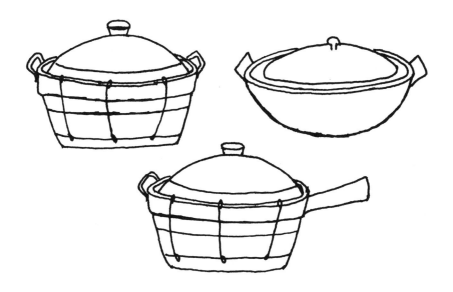

SESAME PINEAPPLE CHICKEN   serves 4 - 6

6 roaster drumsticks (*about 2¾ pounds*) Deboned, p. 121

thumb-size piece of fresh ginger	)
Peeled and crushed	)
1 - 2 scallions Crushed	) Combine.
1 tablespoon ginger wine, p. 16	) Add drumsticks. Mix well.
1 tablespoon regular soy sauce	) Marinate 2 hours if time
4 tablespoons frozen concentrated	) permits or better still over-
pineapple juice	) night in the refrigerator.
½ teaspoon kosher salt or to taste	)
dash of black pepper or to taste	)

½ cup unseasoned dry bread crumbs	) Combine in a plastic bag
2 tablespoons black sesame seeds	) or on a plate.

6 fresh pineapple strips (*about 2- x ¾- x ¾-inch*)

2 - 3 tablespoons flour or *cornstarch*

1 - 2 whole eggs Crack into a deep plate or a large mixing bowl. Beat lightly to combine yolk and white.

1 - 2 tablespoons oil

Chinese parsley or *regular parsley for garnish*

pineapple slices for garnish

maraschino cherries for garnish

(1) Position an oven rack in middle of oven. Preheat oven to 425°.

(2) Drain drumsticks. Place a pineapple strip in center of each. Close opening with toothpicks. Roll in flour, shaking off excess.

(3) Coat with beaten eggs. Roll in bread crumbs mixture to coat evenly all over. Place on a greased rimmed baking sheet or shallow baking pan. Dribble ½ - 1 teaspoon oil over each coated drumstick.

(4) Bake, in middle of oven, uncovered, at 425° for 30 minutes. Turn off oven. Let drumsticks remain in hot oven for 5 minutes.

(5) Remove and discard toothpicks. Arrange cooked drumsticks on a serving platter. Garnish with parsley, pineapple ring and maraschino cherries.

KITCHEN HINT: Canned pineapple chunks can be substituted for the fresh pineapple.

Practical Variations

MUSHROOM & CHINESE SAUSAGE CHICKEN

Substitute: *2 Chinese dried mushrooms (about 1½" in diameter)* and
1 Chinese sausage for the *pineapple*

❶ Soak mushrooms for ½ hour (or longer) to soften. Cut off and discard stems. Cut each cap into 6 strips.

❷ Cut Chinese sausage into ¼'s lengthwise. Cut each length into 3.

❸ Place 2 strips of mushroom and 2 lengths of sausage in center of each deboned drumstick. Close opening with toothpicks.

❹ Continue with Step (3), (4) and (5) on page 120.

PROSCIUTTO & SCALLION CHICKEN

Substitute: *6 strips (2 x ¼ x ¼-inch) prosciutto* and *6 2-inch length white part of scallion* for the *pineapple*

❶ Place 1 strip of prosciutto and 1 length of scallion in center of each deboned drumstick. Close opening with toothpicks.

❷ Continue with Step (3), (4) and (5) on page 120.

Deboning a drumstick:

❶ At the large end of the drumstick, run a sharp knife around the knuckle, between the meat and the bone, cutting as close to the bone as possible.

❷ Push down and pull the meat, inside out, away from the bone. Cut off close at the small end of the drumstick. Save bones for soup or discard.

❸ Turn meat skin side out.

BRASED CHAYOTE CHICKEN

serves 3 - 4

1½ - 2 pounds chicken legs Rinsed. Pat dry. Cut through the bones into
bite-size pieces.

1 tablespoon ginger wine, p. 16	) Combine.
3 slices ginger from ginger wine	) Add chicken. Mix well.
1 tablespoon dark soy sauce	) Marinate 1 hour, if time
1 teaspoon kosher salt or to taste	) permits, or overnight in the
½ teaspoon honey or *sugar*	) refrigerator.

1 small onion Thinly sliced
2 chayotes Peeled. Cut in half lengthwise. Remove and discard seed. Cut into
bite-size chunks.
¼ - ½ cup chicken broth
1 - 2 tablespoons oil

1 teaspoon cornstarch	) Combine in a small bowl.
1 tablespoon water	) Stir just before adding to wok.

(1) Heat wok. Add oil. Swirl to coat wok. Add onion. Stir-fry over high heat until
onion is limp. Add chicken and stir-fry until chicken changes color. Cover
and simmer 10 minutes. Remove chicken to a plate but leave liquid in wok.

(2) Place chayote in a pot. Add liquid from wok to pot. Stir to coat chayote well.
Add broth, if needed, to barely cover chayote. Bring to boil. Cover and
simmer until chayote is tender about 15 - 20 minutes.

(3) Add chicken to chayote. Mix well. Cover. Bring to boil. Simmer until chicken
is cooked. Thicken with cornstarch mixture. Serve hot.

NOTE: Cutting through the bones may result in some small bone chips in the finished dish. If
this a problem, leave legs whole and add during step (2).

KITCHEN HINT: *Mushroom soy sauce* may be substituted for the *dark soy sauce.*

****

Practical Variation

BRAISED CHICKEN WITH CHINESE RADISH

Substitute: *1 - 2 pounds Chinese radish (daikon)* for the *chayotes* Peel
radish. Cut into bite-sized pieces.

Add: *6 - 8 slices fresh ginger* to the pot during step (2).

CHICKEN, SNOW PEAS & BABY CORN   serves 3 - 5

1 pound boneless & skinless chicken breast Cut into about ¼-inch thick slices.

1 teaspoon cornstarch	)
½ teaspoon kosher salt or to taste	) Combine. Stir in chicken.
1 teaspoon sugar	) Marinate ½ hour. Can be done
1 tablespoon ginger wine, p. 16	) the day before and refrigerated.
1 tablespoon regular soy sauce	)

2 slices ginger Fresh or from ginger wine, p. 16
1 scallion Cut into about 1" lengths.
4 - 8 ounces snow peas Stringed
1 can baby corn Drained and rinsed. Cut ears in halves if desired.
few thin slices of carrot
1 teaspoon kosher salt or to taste
3 tablespoons oil
¼ - ½ cup chicken broth

(1) Heat wok. Add 1 tablespoon oil. Swirl to coat wok. Add salt, snow peas, baby corn and carrot. Stir-fry over high heat until snow peas change color, about 2 minutes, adding broth 1 tablespoon at a time if wok is dry. Remove vegetables and any liquid to a clean plate.

(2) Add remaining oil to wok. Add ginger slices and scallion. Stir-fry 10 seconds over high heat. Add chicken. Stir-fry over high heat until chicken changes color, adding broth 1 tablespoon at a time if wok is dry. Remove and discard ginger slices, if desired.

(3) Return vegetables and any liquid to wok. Add additional broth, as needed for gravy. Mix well. Bring to a boil. Serve hot.

****

Practical Variation

CHICKEN WITH BROCCOLI

Substitute: ***Dark*** or ***mushroom soy sauce*** for part of the ***regular soy sauce***
        1 - 1½ pounds broccoli for the ***snow peas*** and ***baby corn*** Cut broccoli into bite-size pieces and blanched, p. 100.

Add: ***¼ - ½ teaspoon Asian chili sauce*** to marinated chicken
        1 - 2 cloves minced garlic

CHICKEN IN HOISIN SAUCE

serves 3 - 5

1 pound boneless & skinless chicken breast Rinsed and pat dry. Cut into about ¾-inch cubes or cut into about ¼-inch thick slices.

1 teaspoon cornstarch	) Combine. Add chicken. Mix well.
1 tablespoon ginger wine, p. 16	) Can be done the day before and
1 tablespoon regular soy sauce	) refrigerated.

1 small red pepper Discard seeds. Cut into about ¾-inch squares.

1 medium green pepper Discard seeds. Cut into about ¾-inch squares.

1 8-ounce can sliced water chestnuts Drained.

4 - 6 ounces fresh mushrooms Cut into about ½-inch thick slices

½ teaspoon kosher salt or to taste

2 - 4 tablespoons hoisin sauce or to taste

½ - ¾ cup roasted unsalted peanuts or **almonds** (sliced or slivered)

2 - 3 tablespoons oil

(1) Heat wok. Add 1 tablespoon oil. Swirl to coat wok. Add salt and vegetables. Stir-fry over high heat for 2 minutes. Remove to a plate.

(2) Add 1 - 2 tablespoons oil to wok. Heat until smoking. Add chicken. Stir-fry over high heat until chicken turns white. Stir in hoisin sauce to taste.

(3) Add vegetables. Stir-fry until chicken is cooked and vegetables reach desired doneness. Stir in nuts and serve.

KITCHEN HINT: For extra gravy add **½ cup of chicken broth** combined with **1 tablespoon cornstarch** before adding nuts.

****

Practical Variations

CHICKEN & TOFU IN HOISIN SAUCE

Use: **½ pound of extra firm tofu** and **½ pound of chicken** instead of **1 pound of chicken** Marinate tofu and chicken separately. Cook chicken first. When chicken turns white, add tofu. Stir-fry until tofu is heated through. Stir in hoisin sauce. Continue with Step (3).

TOFU IN HOISIN SAUCE

Substitute: **1 pound of extra firm tofu** for the **chicken**
1 tablespoon mushroom soy sauce for the **regular soy sauce**

CURRY CHICKEN

2 - 2½ pounds chicken with bones Washed and dried. Cut through bones
  into bite-size pieces.

2 tomatoes Peeled. Cut in half, crosswise. Squeeze out and discard seeds.
  Coarsely chop tomato halves.

2 - 3 potatoes *(preferably red skin)* Peeled. Cut into large chunks.

1 small onion Coarsely chopped.

3 cloves garlic Minced

1 - 2 dried chili peppers (optional) Finely chopped

1 teaspoon kosher salt or to taste

2 - 3 tablespoons curry powder or to taste

3 tablespoons oil *(about)*

1 cup chicken broth or **water**

(1) Heat wok. Add oil. Swirl to coat wok. Add chili pepper, salt and curry
    powder. Stir-fry 5 seconds over medium-high or high heat. Add onion and
    garlic. Stir-fry about 2 minutes or until onion wilts.

(2) Add chicken pieces. Stir-fry over high heat until well coated. Continue stir-
    frying until chicken changes color.

(3) Add tomatoes. Continue stir-frying until chicken is partially cooked. Add
    potatoes and mix well. Transfer all to a pot. Add broth. Bring to a boil. Cover
    and simmer about 45 minutes. Serve hot.

NOTE: Cutting through the bones may result in some small bone chips in the finished dish. If
      this is a problem, use chicken legs and thigh and leave them whole.

KITCHEN HINT: *¼ - 2 teaspoons Asian chili sauce* or *1 - 3 fresh chili peppers*, minced
      may be substituted for the **dried chilies**

KITCHEN HINT: Curry dishes taste better the next day. **Great do-ahead dish.**

****

Practical Variation

CURRY LAMB SHANK

Substitute: **2½ - 3 pounds lamb shank** for the **chicken**

Add: **½ - 1 cup unsweetened coconut milk**
      Simmer an additional 30 - 45 minutes or until lamb is tender.

KITCHEN HINT: Have butcher cut lamb shank into smaller pieces.

STEAMED CHICKEN

serves 3 - 5

1 pound boneless & skinless chicken meat (*preferably thigh meat*) Rinsed.
   Pat dry. Cut into about ¼-inch thick slices.

1 teaspoon kosher salt or to taste)	
½ teaspoon sugar)	Combine in a lightly oiled 9"
¼ teaspoon black or *white pepper*)	pie plate or other heat-proof
1 tablespoon cornstarch)	deep plate. Add chicken, mix
1 tablespoon ginger wine, p. 16)	well. Can be done the day
1 tablespoon regular soy sauce)	before and refrigerated.
2 teaspoons sesame oil (*optional*))	

2 - 4 dried Chinese mushrooms Soak in warm water at least ½ hour to soften.
   Squeeze out excess water. Remove and discard stems. Shred caps.

40 tiger lily flowers Soak in warm water at least ½ hour to soften. Remove and
   discard any hard and woody parts. Cut flowers in halves.

1 tablespoon cloud ears Soak in warm water at least ½ hour to soften.Remove
   and discard any hard and sandy parts. Break large ones into smaller pieces.

15 dried Chinese red dates Washed. Remove and discard seeds. Cut dates
   into thin strips.

1 scallion Thinly sliced

(1) Add mushrooms, tiger lily flowers, cloud ears and red dates to chicken. Mix
   thoroughly.

(2) Steam, p. 15, over high heat for 30 minutes. Sprinkle scallion on top and
   serve.

NOTE: Traditionally, this dish is made using whole chicken, cutting through the bones into bite-
   size pieces. Steamed with the bones attached, the finished dish has a richer flavor. The
   down side is there will be small bone chips so diner has to be very careful when eating. If
   using bone-in chicken, increase amount to 1½ pounds.

KITCHEN HINT: Mushrooms, tiger lily flowers, cloud ears and red dates can be prepared up to a
   day ahead and refrigerated. Add to chicken just before steaming.

BEEF, VEAL & LAMB

128
Stir-fry Beef & Asparagus
Stir-fry Beef, Bok Choy & 3 Peppers
Beef & Curried Cauliflower

129
Beef & Straw Mushrooms
Beef & Portabella Mushrooms

130
Stir-fry Beef & Dried Lotus Root
Stir-fry Lamb & Dried Lotus Root
Stir-fry Chicken & Fresh Lotus Root
Stir-Fry Beef, Tofu & Fresh Lotus Root

132
Beef in Oyster Sauce
Chicken in Oyster Sauce
Tofu in Oyster Sauce
Veal or Lamb in Oyster Sauce
Beef in Hoisin Miso Sauce

134
Stir-fry Beef & Cucumber
Braised Cucumber

135
Beef & Broccoli
Chicken & Broccoli

136
Hoisin Beef with Mushroom Sauce
Hoisin Pork with Mushroom Sauce
Hoisin Chicken with Mushroom Sauce
Hoisin Lamb with Mushroom Sauce

137
Mushroom Sauce
Piquant Mushroom Sauce
Mushroom Sauce with Fennel
Mushroom Sauce with Cherry Tomatoes
Mushroom Sauce with Green Tomatoes

138
Steamed Beef Balls
Steamed Veal Balls

139
Sweet & Sour Meatballs

140
Braised Beef Shank

STIR-FRY BEEF & ASPARAGUS

serves 4 - 6

1 pound flank steak or *sirloin steak* Cut across the grain into about 2 inches wide and ¼-inch thick slices.

1 teaspoon brown or *white sugar*	)
1 teaspoon cornstarch	) Combine.
2 slices ginger from ginger wine, p. 16	) Add beef. Mix well.
1 tablespoon ginger wine, p. 16	) Marinate if time permits.
1 tablespoon regular soy sauce	) Can be done the day
1 tablespoon oil (optional)	) before and refrigerated.
2 teaspoons oyster sauce	)
dash of white pepper or to taste	)

1 pound asparagus Peeled, p. 99. Remove scales if necessary, p. 99. Slant cut into about ½-inch thick slices

1 clove garlic Finely minced

1 - 2 shallots Finely minced

1-inch length white part of scallion Slice into thin rounds

3 - 4 tablespoons oil

½ - 1 teaspoon kosher salt or to taste

¼ - ½ cup chicken broth or as needed

(1) Heat wok. Add 1 tablespoon oil. Swirl to coat wok. Add salt and asparagus. Stir-fry over high heat to a shade under desired doneness, adding 1 tablespoon broth if wok is dry. Remove and arrange on a preheated platter.

(2) Add 2 tablespoons oil to wok. Add garlic and shallots. Stir-fry over high heat for about 30 seconds. Add beef. Stir-fry until beef reaches desired doneness. Add broth as needed for gravy. Arrange on top of asparagus. Garnish with scallion rounds. Serve hot.

****

Practical Variations

STIR-FRY BEEF, BOK CHOY & 3 PEPPERS

Substitute: *1 pound bok choy* for the *asparagus* Slant-cut into about ¼-inch thick slices. Use both stems and leaves.

Add: Few strips each of *red, yellow and green pepper*

BEEF & CURRIED CAULIFLOWER

Substitute: *1 pound cauliflower* for the *asparagus* Cut into bite-sized pieces.

Add: *1 - 3 teaspoons curry powder* during step (1).

BEEF & STRAW MUSHROOMS serves 3 - 5

1 pound flank steak or ***sirloin steak*** Cut across the grain into about 2 inches wide and ¼-inch thick slices.

1 teaspoon brown or ***white sugar***	)
1 teaspoon cornstarch	) Combine.
2 teaspoons mushroom soy sauce	) Add beef. Mix well.
2 teaspoons regular soy sauce	) Marinate if time permits.
white or ***black pepper or to taste***	) Can be done the day
1 tablespoon ginger wine, p.16	) before and refrigerated.
2 slices ginger from ginger wine, p. 16	)
1 tablespoon oil (optional)	)

1 can peeled or ***unpeeled straw mushrooms*** Rinsed and drained
1 can baby corn Rinsed and drained. Leave whole or cut in halves.
½ - 1 green pepper Cut into strips or squares
1 small onion Peeled and quartered
¼ - ½ cup carrot slices
2 or more cloves garlic Minced
½ - 1 teaspoon kosher salt or to taste
3 - 4 tablespoons oil
¼ - ½ cup chicken broth or as needed

(1) Heat wok. Add 1 tablespoon oil. Swirl to coat wok. Add salt, garlic and vegetables. Stir-fry over high heat for about 2 minutes or until vegetables are heated through, adding broth 1 tablespoon at a time if wok is dry. Remove vegetables to a platter.

(2) Add 2 - 3 tablespoons oil to wok. Heat until smoking. Add beef. Stir-fry over high heat until reached desired doneness, adding broth 1 tablespoon at a time, if needed, to prevent burning. Stir in vegetables and additional broth, if desired, for gravy. Bring to boil. Serve hot.

****

Practical Variation

BEEF & PORTABELLA MUSHROOMS

Substitute: ***½ - ¾ pound portabella mushrooms*** for the ***straw mushrooms***
　　　　　　Cut portabella mushrooms into about ½-inch thick slices.
Add:　　　***Asian chili sauce*** or ***minced fresh chili peppers*** to taste

STIR-FRY BEEF & DRIED LOTUS ROOT serves 3 - 4

4 - 5 slices dried lotus root Soak in cold water at least 2 hours, preferably overnight. Slice crosswise as thinly as possible (see kitchen hint, p. 131). Keep slices soaked in cold water until ready to use

½ pound flank steak or ***sirloin steak*** Cut across the grain into about 2 inches wide and ¼-inch thick slices.

¼ teaspoon kosher salt or to taste	) Combine.
½ teaspoon brown or ***white sugar***	) Add beef. Mix well.
1 teaspoon cornstarch	) Marinate if time
2 slices fresh ginger from ginger wine, p. 16	) permits.
2 teaspoons ginger wine, p. 16	) Can be done the
2 teaspoons regular soy sauce	) day before and
2 teaspoons oil (optional)	) refrigerated.

1 - 3 cloves garlic Minced
few carrot slices
1 medium onion Peeled. Sliced thinly.
1 scallion Shredded or thinly sliced, both green and white parts.
2 - 4 tablespoons oil
¾ - 1 cup chicken broth or as needed
¼ teaspoon sugar (optional)
1 tablespoon oyster sauce
white or ***black pepper to taste***

(1) Heat wok. Add 1 - 2 tablespoons oil. Swirl to coat wok. Add garlic. Stir-fry over medium-high heat for about 30 seconds. Add beef. Stir-fry over high heat until color changes. Remove to a clean plate.

(2) Add 1 - 2 tablespoons oil to wok. Drain lotus root and add to wok. Stir-fry over medium-high heat, adding broth 1 - 2 tablespoons at a time as you stir-fry. When nearly all the broth is absorbed, stir in carrot, onion, sugar, oyster sauce and white pepper. Mix well.

(3) Stir in beef. Stir-fry until beef reaches desired doneness. Transfer to serving platter. Sprinkle scallion on top. Serve hot.

NOTE: 1 - 3 sections (¾ - 1 pound) fresh lotus root may be substituted for the dried lotus root. Peel fresh lotus root and slice, crosswise, thinly.

Practical Variations

STIR-FRY LAMB & DRIED LOTUS ROOT

Substitute: _½ pound boneless lamb leg meat_ for the _beef_

Add: _1 - 3 teaspoons curry powder_ same time as _garlic_

        ¼ - 1 teaspoon Asian chili sauce or _1 - 2 minced fresh chili peppers_ same time as _garlic_

STIR-FRY CHICKEN & FRESH LOTUS ROOT

Substitute: _½ pound boneless & skinless chicken meat_ for the _beef_

        1 - 3 sections fresh lotus root for the _dried lotus root_ Peeled. Sliced, crosswise, thinly. Submerge in cold water until ready to use.

Add: _¼ - 1 teaspoon Asian chili sauce_ or _1 - 2 minced fresh chili peppers_ Add during step (3).

STIR-FRY BEEF, TOFU & FRESH LOTUS ROOT

Substitute: _¼ - ½ pound extra-firm tofu_ for _¼ pound of beef_ Cut tofu into about ¼-inch thick bite-sized pieces.

        1 - 3 sections fresh lotus root for the _dried lotus root_ Peeled. Sliced, crosswise, thinly. Submerge in cold water until ready to use.

Add: _¼ - 1 teaspoon Asian chili sauce_ or _1 - 2 minced fresh chili pepper_ Add during step (3).

KITCHEN HINT: Fresh lotus root is quite hard. Use a sharp knife to avoid cutting oneself. You may wish to slice through the section lengthwise first then slice thinly crosswise.

KITCHEN HINT: To slice dried lotus root into paper-thin slices: Place soaked lotus root flat on cutting board. Hold a very sharp cleaver or knife parallel to the lotus root and slice across.

KITCHEN HINT: Cook lotus root in a non-reactive cookware. If cooked in carbon steel, spun steel or cast iron cookware, lotus root will turn gray-black. Still edible.

KITCHEN HINT: To prevent insects from attacking dried lotus roots, place dried lotus roots in a container, I prefer a glass container. Add 2 or more bay leaves, cover with a tight fitting lid. This works also for all other dried ingredients like beans, pasta, rice, flour, mushrooms, dates, tiger lily flowers, etc.

BEEF IN OYSTER SAUCE

serves 3 - 5

1 pound flank steak or *sirloin steak* Cut across the grain into about 2 inches wide and ¼-inch thick slices.

½ teaspoon kosher salt or to taste	) Combine.
1 teaspoon brown or *white sugar*	) Add beef. Mix well.
1½ teaspoons cornstarch	) Marinate if time
3 slices fresh ginger from ginger wine, p. 16	) permits.
1 tablespoon ginger wine, p. 16	) Can be done the
1 tablespoon regular soy sauce	) day before and
1 tablespoon oil (optional)	) refrigerated.

1 medium onion Peeled. Cut in half lengthwise and sliced thinly.
1 - 2 carrots Peeled. Cut into thin slices.
2 - 4 broccoli stems Peeled. Cut into about ¼-inch thick slices.
½ - 1 can straw mushrooms Rinsed and drained.
1 scallion Shredded or thinly sliced, both green and white parts.
2 or more cloves garlic Minced
½ teaspoon kosher salt or to taste
3 - 4 tablespoons oil
3 - 4 tablespoons chicken broth or as needed

1 teaspoon cornstarch	)
¼ cup chicken broth or *water*	) Combine in a small bowl.
2 tablespoons oyster sauce	) This is the sauce.
white or *black pepper to taste*	) Stir well just before adding to wok.
¼ teaspoon sugar	)

(1) Heat wok. Add 1 tablespoon oil. Swirl to coat wok. Add salt, carrots, broccoli stems and mushrooms. Stir-fry over medium-high heat for about 3 minutes or until vegetables reach desired doneness, adding broth 1 tablespoon at a time if wok is dry. Remove vegetables to a plate.

(2) Add 2 - 3 tablespoons oil to wok. Add onion and garlic, stir-fry over high heat until wilted. Add beef. Stir-fry until beef reaches desired doneness, adding broth 1 tablespoon at a time if wok is dry.

(3) Stir in vegetables and sauce. Bring to a boil. Mix well. Transfer to serving platter. Sprinkle scallion on top. Serve hot.

Practical Variations

CHICKEN IN OYSTER SAUCE

Substitute: *1 pound boneless & skinless chicken meat* for the *beef*
mushroom soy sauce for the *regular soy sauce*
4 - 8 ounces of portabella mushrooms for the *straw mushrooms* Cut portabella mushrooms into about ½-inch thick slices.

Add: *¼ - 2 teaspoons Asian chili sauce* to sauce

TOFU IN OYSTER SAUCE

Substitute: *1 pound extra firm tofu* for the *beef*
dark or *mushroom soy sauce* for the *regular soy sauce*
½ - 1 each red, green and yellow pepper for the *carrot and broccoli* Cut peppers into about 1-inch squares.
4 - 6 ounces small button mushrooms for the *straw mushrooms* Leave button mushrooms whole or cut in halves.

VEAL OR LAMB IN OYSTER SAUCE

Substitute: *1 pound veal* or *lamb leg meat* for the *beef*
½ tablespoon dark or *mushroom soy sauce* for *½ tablespoon regular soy sauce*

BEEF IN HOISIN MISO SAUCE

Substitute: *1 tablespoon hoisin sauce* and *1 tablespoon miso* for the *oyster sauce*

KITCHEN HINT: The following may be substituted for the broccoli stems
1 - 2 ribs celery Slant-cut celery into about ¼-inch thick slices
*4 - 8 ounces canned sliced water chestnut*s Drained
*8 - 10 ounces fresh water chestnut*s Peeled and sliced
6 - 8 ounces jicama Peeled and sliced
6 - 8 ounces sunchoke (Jerusalem artichoke) Peeled and sliced.
KITCHEN HINT: Substitute *4 - 8 ounces of any kind of fresh mushrooms* for the *straw mushrooms.*

STIR-FRY BEEF & CUCUMBER

serves 2 - 4

½ pound flank steak or *sirloin steak* Cut across the grain into about 2 inches wide and ¼-inch thick slices.

¼ teaspoon kosher salt or to taste	) Combine.
½ teaspoon brown or *white sugar*	) Add beef. Mix well.
1 teaspoon cornstarch	) Marinate if time
2 slices fresh ginger from ginger wine, p. 16	) permits.
2 teaspoons ginger wine, p. 16	) Can be done the
2 teaspoons mushroom soy sauce	) day before and
2 teaspoons oil (optional)	) refrigerated.

1 - 2 cucumbers Peeled, cut in half, lengthwise. Remove and discard seeds. Slant-cut into about ½-inch thick slices.

few strips red pepper (optional)

2 - 3 scallions Cleaned. Cut into 1-inch lengths, both green and white parts.

½ teaspoon cornstarch	)
1 tablespoon water	) Combine in a small bowl.
1 tablespoon oyster sauce	) Mix well just before adding to wok.
white or *black pepper to taste*	)

3 tablespoons oil
¼ teaspoon salt or to taste
3 - 4 tablespoons chicken broth or as needed

(1) Heat wok. Add 1 - 2 tablespoons oil. Swirl to coat wok. Add scallions. Stir-fry over medium-high heat for about 30 seconds. Add beef. Stir-fry over high heat until beef color changes. Remove to a plate.

(2) Add 1 tablespoon oil to wok, if needed. Add salt, cucumber and red pepper. Stir-fry using high heat, until cucumber is just heated through.

(3) Add beef. Stir-fry until beef reaches desired doneness. Add broth as needed for gravy. Stir in cornstarch mixture. Mix well. Serve hot.

NOTE: Many people who are allergic to cucumber find cooked cucumber agreeable.
****

BRAISED CUCUMBER (Gardeners: This is a great recipe for using the missed cucumber that turned yellow.)

Cucumber

❶ Peeled. Cut in ½ lengthwise. Discard seeds. Cut into slices or chunks.

❷ Stir-fry in oil or butter to desired doneness or braise in broth until soft.

❸ Add onions, shallots, garlic and/or other herbs and spices for flavor.

BEEF & BROCCOLI

serves 3 - 5

1 pound flank or *sirloin steak* Cut across the grain into about ¼-inch thick
slices.

1 teaspoon cornstarch	)
1 teaspoon brown or *white sugar*	) Combine. Add beef. Mix well.
1 tablespoon ginger wine, p. 16	) Marinate, if time permits.
1 tablespoon regular soy sauce	) Can be done the day before
1 tablespoon oil (optional)	) and refrigerated.
dash of white pepper or to taste	)

1 bunch broccoli Cut florets into bite-sized pieces. Peel stem and slant-cut
into bite-sized pieces. Place all in a large container. Pour on boiling water
to cover. Stir and drain. Cool under cold running water. Drain again.

1 small onion Peeled. Cut in half and slice thinly lengthwise.

2 - 6 whole dried chili peppers

3 - 4 tablespoons oil

½ - 1 teaspoon kosher salt or to taste

¼ - ½ cup chicken broth or as needed

(1) Heat wok. Add 1 tablespoon oil. Swirl to coat wok. Add salt, broccoli and
onion. Stir-fry over high heat until reached desired doneness, about 2
minutes, adding broth 1 tablespoon at a time if wok is dry. Remove to a
plate.

(2) Add 2 tablespoons oil to wok. Heat until smoking. Add whole chilies, stir-fry
10 seconds or until chilies turn black. Add beef. Stir-fry, over high heat,
until reach desired doneness, adding broth 1 tablespoon at a time if wok is
dry. Add broccoli and additional broth for gravy. Bring to a boil. Serve hot.

NOTE: DO NOT eat whole chilies.

****

Practical Variations

CHICKEN & BROCCOLI

Substitute: *1 pound boneless & skinless chicken breast* for the *beef*
dark or *mushroom soy sauce* for the *regular soy sauce*

HOISIN BEEF WITH MUSHROOM SAUCE serves 4 - 6

2 pounds ½-inch (about) thick boneless chuck top blade steaks

1 teaspoon kosher salt or to taste	)
1 tablespoon sugar	) Combine. This is the
2 tablespoons ginger wine, p. 16	) marinade. Add beef.
4 slices ginger from ginger wine, p. 16	) Marinate, if possible,
1 tablespoon hoisin sauce	) at least 2 hours or
1 tablespoon dark or mushroom soy sauce	) overnight in the
2 tablespoons oil (optional)	) refrigerator.
2 - 3 cloves garlic Minced	)

Mushroom sauce, p. 137
Chinese parsley or curly parsley (optional) for garnish

(1) Position an oven rack in middle of oven. Preheat broiler.
(2) Arrange beef, in one layer, leaving a little space between each piece, on broiler grid or on a rack over a baking pan.
(3) Broil on high for 6 minutes. Turn. Broil 5 - 7 minutes more or until reached desired doneness. Arrange on a preheated platter.
(4) While beef is broiling, make Mushroom Sauce, p. 137.
(5) Spoon mushroom sauce over broiled beef. Garnish with parsley. Serve hot.

NOTE: Mushroom soy sauce unavailable? Substitute *dark soy sauce* or *regular soy sauce*.
****

Practical Variations

HOISIN PORK WITH MUSHROOM SAUCE

Substitute: *2 pounds ½-inch thick pork chops (with or without bone)* for the *chuck top blade steaks*

HOISIN CHICKEN WITH MUSHROOM SAUCE

Substitute: *2 pounds boneless chicken breast* for the *chuck top blade steaks* Flatten chicken breast, with a mallet, to even thickness.

HOISIN LAMB WITH MUSHROOM SAUCE

Substitute: *2 pounds ½-inch thick lamb chops* for the *chuck top blade steaks*

MUSHROOM SAUCE

½ pound fresh mushrooms Washed. Chopped coarsely or sliced thinly
1 medium onion Sliced thinly
1 - 2 cloves garlic Minced
1 teaspoon kosher salt or to taste
Juice from broiler pan
¼ - ½ cup chicken or *beef broth*
1 tablespoon oil

2 teaspoons cornstarch)	Combine in a small bowl.
1 tablespoon water)	Stir well just before adding to saucepan.

(1) Heat saucepan. Add oil, onion and garlic. Stir-fry over medium heat until onion wilts. Add mushrooms. Stir-fry until mushrooms wilt.

(2) Add salt, juice from broiler pan and broth, as needed for gravy. Bring to boil. Thicken with cornstarch mixture.

KITCHEN HINT: Combine 2 or more varieties of mushrooms for a different and interesting flavor.

****

Practical Variations

PIQUANT MUSHROOM SAUCE
Add: *1 - 3 red* and/or *green hot chili peppers*, sliced or coarsely chopped, during step (1)

MUSHROOM SAUCE WITH FENNEL
Add: *1 cup thinly sliced fennel* during step (1)

MUSHROOM SAUCE WITH CHERRY TOMATOES
Add: *6 - 8 red* and *yellow cherry tomatoes,* cut in halves, during step (2)

MUSHROOM SAUCE WITH GREEN TOMATOES
Add: *½ - 1 cup thinly sliced green tomatoes* during step (1)
    2 - 4 teaspoons sugar or to taste during step (2)

STEAMED BEEF BALLS

serves 4 - 6

1 cup glutinous rice Rinsed and soaked 2 - 3 hours. Drain just before using.
1 pound lean ground beef
1 red skin potato (about 6 ounces) Peeled.

2 eggs Lightly beaten.	)
1 small onion Minced.	) Combine in a large mixing
1½ teaspoons kosher salt or to taste	) bowl.
1 teaspoon sugar	) This is the egg mixture.
1 tablespoon ginger wine, p. 16	)
1 tablespoon regular soy sauce	)

2 tablespoons regular soy sauce	)
1 - 2 tablespoons rice vinegar	) Combine in a small serving
¼ - 1 teaspoon Asian chili sauce	) bowl. This is the dipping sauce.
or *minced fresh chilies*	)

1 - 2 pounds shredded nappa cabbage

(1) Shred potato, using a box grater, into egg mixture. Mix well. Add beef. Combine well, but do not overmix.

(2) Add water to steamer base. Add steamer rack or steamer basket. Line with shredded nappa cabbage. Bring water to boil. Steam cabbage until wilted.

(3) Gently shape meat mixture into meatballs, using about 1 tablespoon mixture. Roll in drained rice to coat completely.

(4) Place shaped meatballs on cabbage, leaving a little space between each.

(5) Steam, covered, over high heat for 30 minutes. Serve hot with sauce. Can be done the day before. Reheat by steaming for 5 - 10 minutes.

NOTE: *½ cup mashed potato* can be substituted for the *red skin potato*

KITCHEN HINT: Spoon any leftover rice onto cabbage. Steam same as meatballs.
KITCHEN HINT: Steamed meatballs freeze well. Make extra for the freezer. Reheat by steaming or in the microwave.

****

Practical Variations

STEAMED VEAL BALLS

Substitute: *1 pound ground veal* for the *ground beef*
Add: *2 - 4 tablespoons finely chopped cilantro* to *potato mixture*

SWEET & SOUR MEATBALLS

serves 4 - 6

1 pound lean ground beef

1 egg Lightly beaten	)
¼ cup milk	)
5 tablespoons unseasoned dry bread crumbs	) Combine. Add
1 teaspoon sugar	) beef. Mix well.
1 teaspoon kosher salt or to taste	) Can be done the
1 tablespoon regular soy sauce	) day before and
1 tablespoon ginger wine, p. 16	) refrigerated.
1 scallion, white & green parts Minced	)
¼ teaspoon white or *black pepper or to taste*	)

1 tablespoon cornstarch	)
1 tablespoon ginger wine, p. 16	)
2 tablespoons white vinegar	) Combine in a large, non-reactive
¼ cup sugar	) saucepan.
¼ cup regular soy sauce	) This is the sweet & sour sauce.
¼ cup tomato sauce	)
½ cup water	)

1 - 2 cups frozen peas & carrots Thawed

(1) Position an oven rack in middle of oven. Preheat oven to 400°.
(2) Make meatballs the size of walnuts. Place on lightly oiled baking pan.
(3) Bake, uncovered, in 400° oven for 20 minutes.
(4) Bring sweet & sour sauce to boil, stirring constantly. Add meatballs and peas & carrots. Bring to boil. Simmer until meatballs and peas & carrots are heated through. Serve hot with lots of rice.

KITCHEN HINT: *Sweet peppers, celery, onion or other vegetables* of choice may be substituted for the *peas & carrots.*
KITCHEN HINT: Cooked meatballs freeze well. Make extra for the freezer.
To freeze: Cool. Package in freezer container or freezer bag. Label, date and freeze.

BRAISED BEEF SHANK

serves 6 - 8

3 pounds 1-inch (about) thick bone-in beef shank Trim away any fat.
3 - 4 cloves garlic Minced
2 scallions Cleaned. Sliced thinly.
6 - 8 slices of ginger from ginger wine, p. 16

2 whole star anise)	Tie in a piece of cheesecloth or place in a metal
4 - 5 peppercorns)	tea ball.

walnut-size piece of Chinese rock sugar or *1 tablespoon brown sugar*
1 teaspoon kosher salt or to taste
¼ cup dark or *mushroom soy sauce*
¼ cup ginger wine, p. 16
3 cups chicken or *beef broth* or *water*
2 tablespoons oil
1½ - 2 pounds Chinese radish (daikon) Peeled. Cut into about 1-inch chunks.

(1) Place whole piece of shank on broiler pan, brush lightly with oil. Broil in the middle of oven for 7 minutes or until lightly browned. Turn and broil the other side for 5 - 7 minutes or until lightly browned.

(2) Heat a 4-quart or larger pot. Add 1 tablespoon oil. Add garlic, scallions and ginger slices. Stir-fry until garlic is lightly browned. Add broth, star anise, peppercorns, sugar, salt, soy sauce and ginger wine. Bring to a boil.

(3) Add broiled shank. Bring to a boil. Cover and boil, using medium low heat, for 30 minutes. Remove shank. Cool slightly. Cut into about 1-inch cubes. Return to pot, including bones. Cover and boil, using medium low heat, another 30 minutes.

(4) Add Chinese radish. Bring to a boil. Cover and cook, using medium low heat, 30 - 45 minutes or until meat is tender and radish is soft.

(5) Remove meat and radish. Reduce sauce, if necessary, using high heat. There should be about 1½ cup. Remove surface fat. Adjust taste. Pour over meat and radish. Serve hot.

KITCHEN HINT: This dish freezes well. Double recipe (but not Chinese radish). At the end of step (3), remove half of the meat and liquid. Cool, place in freezer container or freezer bag, date, label and freeze.

PORK

SPARERIBS WITH PRESERVED PLUMS   serves 2 - 4

1 pound small spareribs or country-style spareribs Cut into bite-sized
   pieces.
2 cloves garlic Minced
1 scallion Cleaned and thinly sliced, both green and white parts.
4 - 7 preserved plums Mashed using a fork
1 tablespoon crushed Chinese rock sugar or *light brown sugar*
1 tablespoon cornstarch
1 tablespoon ginger wine, p. 16
2 teaspoons dark, mushroom or *regular soy sauce*
dash of white pepper or to taste

(1) Combine all of the above in a lightly oiled 9-inch heatproof pie plate or other
   heatproof deep dish.
(2) Bring water in steamer base to boil. Place plate of ribs on steamer rack or
   steamer basket.
(3) Steam over high heat for 45 - 50 minutes. Serve hot.

NOTE: Preserved plums, called "suan mei" in Chinese, are whole plums, including seeds, preserved in brine. These light brown plums range in sizes from large, about 1½-inch long,
   to small, about ¾-inch long. Quite salty and sour. Use the lesser quantity for the large
   plums and the larger quantity for the small plums.

KITCHEN HINT: This dish tastes better if made the day before. Steam for 15 minutes to reheat.
   Great do-ahead dish.

NOTE: Please read about **Steaming,** p. 15.

****

Practical Variations

CHICKEN WINGS WITH PRESERVED PLUMS

Substitute: *1 pound middle section of chicken wings* for the *spareribs*
Add: *Fresh chili pepper* (*optional*) Thinly sliced or minced

SPARERIBS IN BLACK BEAN SAUCE

serves 2 - 4

1 pound small pork spareribs Cut into bite-sized pieces.
2 - 3 slices ginger from ginger wine, p. 16
1 - 3 chili peppers, fresh or *dried* Remove and discard seeds. Minced
2 tablespoons fermented black beans Rinsed and drained
1 - 3 cloves garlic Minced
¼ teaspoon salt or to taste
2 tablespoons oil
1 teaspoon sugar
1 teaspoon dark soy sauce
1 teaspoon regular soy sauce
2 tablespoons ginger wine, p. 16
½ - ¾ cup chicken or pork broth

2 teaspoons cornstarch)	Combine in a small bowl.
1 tablespoon water)	Stir well just before adding to saucepan.

(1) Heat wok. Add oil. Swirl to coat wok. Add ginger, chili peppers, fermented black beans, garlic and salt. Stir-fry over medium-high heat until fragrant, about 2 minutes.

(2) Add spareribs. Stir fry over high heat until meat changes color. Add sugar, dark soy sauce, regular soy sauce and ginger wine. Stir-fry until all the liquid is absorbed.

(3) Drain and discard excess oil while transferring spareribs to a saucepan. Add broth. Bring to boil. Cover and simmer until ribs are tender, about 45 minutes. Thicken with cornstarch mixture. Serve hot.

****

Practical Variations

CHICKEN WINGS IN BLACK BEAN SAUCE
Substitute: *1 pound chicken wings* for the *spareribs* Separate wings at joints.

LAMB RIBS IN BLACK BEAN SAUCE
Substitute: *1 pound lamb ribs* for the *spareribs* Cut into bite-sized pieces.

PRESSED TOFU IN BLACK BEAN SAUCE
Substitute: *1 pound firm tofu* for the *spareribs* Drained. Wrap in layers of paper towels or a clean kitchen towel. Refrigerate overnight. Cut into bite-sized pieces. Simmer only 5 minutes during step (3).

SWEET & SOUR PORK

serves 4 - 6

1 pound lean pork Cut into about ¾-inch cubes	)
1 egg yolk	) Combine.
½ teaspoon kosher salt or to taste	) Marinate ½ hour
1 tablespoon cornstarch	) or overnight in the
1 tablespoon regular soy sauce	) refrigerator.
1 tablespoon cold water	)

¼ cup flour	) Combine on a plate or wax paper.
¼ cup cornstarch	) This is the coating for the pork.

¼ cup sugar	)
¼ cup regular soy sauce	)
¼ cup tomato sauce	) Combine in a small bowl.
1 tablespoon ginger wine, p. 16	) This is the sauce.
2 tablespoons white vinegar	)
½ cup water	)

1 tablespoon cornstarch	) Combine in a small bowl.
2 tablespoons water	) Stir well before adding to wok.

1 carrot Peeled. Roll cut. Parboil 5 minutes. Drain and cool under cold running water. Drain again.

1 8-ounce can bamboo shoot chunks Drained and rinsed. Cut into wedges about the same size as carrot.

1 large onion Peeled. Cut into about 1½-inch chunks.

1 8-ounce can chunk-style pineapple Drained

1 large green pepper Remove and discard seeds and membrane. Cut into about 1½-inch squares.

3 - 4 cups oil for deep frying

1 tablespoon oil

(1) In a wok or 3-quart saucepan, heat oil for deep frying to 375°.

(2) Coat pork cubes with flour mixture, shaking off excess. Deep fry, a ¼ at a time, until golden, about 5 - 6 minutes. Remove from oil and drain on paper towels. Repeat with remaining pork.

(3) Heat a clean wok. Add 1 tablespoon oil. Swirl to coat wok. Add carrots, bamboo shoots, onion and pineapple. Stir-fry over high heat for 2 minutes.

SWEET & SOUR PORK (continued)

(4) Add sauce mixture. Bring to a boil. Simmer 1 minute.

(5) Thicken with cornstarch mixture. Stir in fried pork and green pepper. Serve hot with lots of rice.

KITCHEN HINT: If you prefer your peppers cooked, add them during step (3).

NOTE: Please read about **Deep-frying**, p. 14.

****

Practical Variations

SWEET AND SOUR CHICKEN
Substitute: *1 pound boneless and skinless chicken meat* for the *pork* Cut chicken into about ¾-inch cubes

SWEET AND SOUR SHRIMP
Substitute: *1½ pound shrimp* for the *pork* Shell shrimp but leave tail on. Devein. Wash. Pat dry. Butterfly, p. 35
1 egg white for the *egg yolk*

SWEET AND SOUR TOFU
Substitute: *1 pound firm tofu* for the *pork* Cut tofu into about ¾-inch cubes
1 whole egg for the *egg yolk*

SWEET AND SOUR MEATBALLS
Substitute: *Any kind of meatballs (or use the **Pork Meatballs** recipe, p. 146)* for the *pork*
Eliminate: *Flour & cornstarch mixture*
Prepare: *1½ times the sauce*
Cooking: ❶ Skip steps (1) and (2) on page 144.
❷ Continue with step (3) on page 144 and steps (4) and (5) above.

PORK MEATBALLS

1 pound ground pork	)
1 egg Lightly beaten	) Combine well. Form
4 tablespoons tapioca starch or *cornstarch*	) into meatballs about
1 tablespoon ginger wine, p . 16	) 1-inch in diameter.
1 tablespoon regular soy sauce	) Bake on a lightly
1½ tablespoons minced shallots or *scallion*	) oiled baking pan,
½ - 1 teaspoon kosher salt	) in 350º preheated
½ teaspoon sugar	) oven, for 20 - 25
dash of white or *black pepper or to taste*	) minutes.
1 teaspoon Asian sesame oil (optional)	)

TURKEY MEATBALLS

Substitute: *Ground turkey* for the *ground pork*

4 tablespoons flour for the *tapioca starch*

Dark or mushroom soy sauce for the *regular soy sauce*

3 MEATS MEATBALLS

Use: *⅓ pound ground beef, ⅓ pound ground veal* and *⅓ pound ground pork* instead of *1 pound ground pork*

NOTE: Baked meatballs freeze well. Make extra for the freezer.

KITCHEN HINT: Left with a small quantity of meat mixture that is not worth putting on the baking pan to bake? Use as follows:

Meatcake: Spread meat mixture in a preheated, oiled frying pan to about ¼-inch thickness. Cook until golden. Turn and brown the other side. Cool and cut into bite-sized strips. Use in stir-fry.

Boiled Meatballs: In a 3- to 4-quart saucepan, bring 5 - 6 cups water to boil. Add meatballs, simmer until meatballs float to the surface. Simmer another 5 minutes or until meatballs are cooked through. Use in soups, stir-fries, stews, marinara sauce or freeze for another day.

Or add uncooked meatballs directly to boiling broth. Add some vegetables and some cooked pasta for a hearty soup.

PORK & SPAGHETTI SQUASH
serves 3 - 4

1 pound spaghetti squash Peeled. Remove and discard seeds. Cut into 2 or 3 large chunks. Parboil 10 - 15 minutes, should still be crunchy. Cool under cold running water. Drain. Separate into strands. Can be done the day before and refrigerated.

½ pound lean pork Shredded	)
1 tablespoon ginger wine, p. 16	) Combine and marinate.
1 tablespoon hoisin sauce	) Can be done the day before and
1 tablespoon regular soy sauce	) refrigerated.
1 teaspoon sugar	)

2 Chinese pork sausages Shredded
4 ounces snow peas Stringed and shredded
1 medium red onion Thinly sliced
1 teaspoon salt or to taste
2 - 3 tablespoons oil
½ - 1 cup chicken broth

1 teaspoon cornstarch	) Combine in a small bowl.
1 tablespoon water	) Stir well just before adding to wok.

(1) Heat wok or frying pan. Add 1 - 3 teaspoons oil and Chinese sausage. Stir-fry over medium heat until some of the fat is rendered. Add pork. Stir-fry over high heat until pork changes color. Remove to a plate.

(2) Add 2 tablespoons oil to wok. Add salt and onion. Stir-fry over medium-high to high heat for about 1 minute. Add squash and snow peas. Stir-fry until snow peas change color, about 1 minute. Add pork and Chinese sausage. Mix well.

(3) Stir in broth. Bring to a boil. Cover and simmer about 2 minutes or until squash is heated through and pork is cooked. Thicken with cornstarch mixture. Serve hot.

****

Practical Variations

PORK & ZUCCHINI
Substitute: ***1 pound zucchini*** for the ***spaghetti squash*** Shredded.

KITCHEN HINT: Lack of time? Slice the ingredients instead of shredding.

MU SHU PORK

serves 3 - 4

½ pound lean pork Shredded)	
¼ teaspoon sugar)	
1 teaspoon cornstarch)	Combine. Mix well. Can be done
2 teaspoons regular soy sauce)	the day before and refrigerated.
1 teaspoon dark soy sauce)	
1 tablespoon ginger wine, p. 16)	

½ cup shredded bamboo shoots

¼ cup packed (about 40) tiger lily flowers Soak in water at least ½ hour to soften. Remove and discard any hard and woody parts. Cut in half.

2 tablespoons cloud ears Soak in water at least ½ hour to soften. Remove and discard any sandy and woody parts. Break into small pieces.

4 - 5 scallions Cleaned. Shredded or slant cut, both white and green parts.

4 large eggs Lightly beaten

4 - 5 tablespoons oil

1½ teaspoons kosher salt or to taste

1 - 2 teaspoons sesame oil (optional)

2 - 3 tablespoons broth or as needed

steamed Chinese pancakes, p. 65

2 - 3 tablespoons hoisin Place in a small condiment dish.

(1) Heat wok. Add 1 tablespoon oil. Swirl to coat wok. Add eggs. Scramble until just set. Transfer to a plate. Cut into small pieces.

(2) Add 2 tablespoons oil to wok. Heat to near smoking. Add pork. Stir-fry over high heat until color changes. Remove to a plate.

(3) Add 1 tablespoon oil to wok. Add salt, bamboo shoots, tiger lily flowers and cloud ears. Stir-fry about 2 minutes, adding broth, 1 tablespoon at a time, if wok seems dry.

(4) Add pork and scallion. Stir-fry until pork is cooked. Mix in eggs. Stir in sesame oil. Serve with steamed Chinese pancakes. (See page 149 How to assemble Mu Shu Pork.)

Practical Variations

Mu Shu Chicken In Steamed Pita Pockets

Substitute: *½ pound boneless and skinless chicken breast* for the *pork*
½ cup shredded water chestnuts for the *bamboo shoots*
1 - 2 cups 2-inch lengths Chinese chives for the *scallion*
Steamed small pita halves for the *Chinese pancakes*

Add: *3 - 4 lettuce leaves, green* or *red* Tear into 2 - 4 smaller pieces.

To steam pita: Cut pita into 2 half-circles. Add water to steamer base. Place steamer rack or steamer basket in steamer base. Line with a damp steamer cloth or cheesecloth. Bring water to a boil. Place pita halves on damp cloth, may overlap, cover and steam on high heat for 5 - 10 minutes or until pita is pliable.

To serve: Brush inside of pita with a bit of hoisin sauce. Tuck in a piece of lettuce leaf. Fill with chicken mixture. Enjoy.

How to assemble Mu Shu Pork:

❶ Spread a steamed pancake, browned side down, on a plate. Brush a thin layer of hoisin sauce on center of pancake.

❷ Spoon about 2 tablespoons meat mixture on top of hoisin sauce.

❸ Fold lower side of pancake over filling.

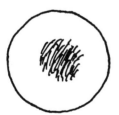  

❹ Fold right side of pancake over.

❺ Fold upper side of pancake down.

❻ Pick up wrapped pancake with fingers. Eat starting at open end.

CUCUMBER LOGS

serves 4 - 5

3 - 5 cucumbers Peeled. Cut into 1-inch - 1½-inch long logs. From one end, remove seeds leaving a thin layer of seeds at the opposite end.

¾ pound lean ground pork	)
4 ounces raw shrimp Shelled. Deveined. Chopped finely	)
2 - 3 Chinese dried mushrooms Soak in water at	) Combine.
least ½ hour to soften. Remove and discard stems.	) Fill
Chop caps finely.	) hollowed
1 scallion Cleaned. Chopped finely, white and green parts	) out
1 egg Lightly beaten.	) cucumber
1 teaspoon salt or to taste	) logs with
1 teaspoon sugar	) this meat
1 tablespoon cornstarch	) mixture.
1 tablespoon regular soy sauce	)
1 tablespoon ginger wine, p. 16	)

A few carrot slices
A few cloud ears *(optional)* Soak in water at least ½ hour to soften. Remove and discard any woody and sandy parts.
A few tiger lily flowers *(optional)* Soak in water at least ½ hour to soften. Remove and discard any woody parts. Tie each into a knot (optional).
4 - 5 tablespoons oil
½ - 1 cup chicken broth
Salt to taste

2 teaspoons cornstarch	) Combine in a small bowl.
1 tablespoon water	) Stir well just before adding to frying pan.

(1) Heat a 10 - 12-inch frying pan. Add oil. Swirl to coat the entire cooking surface. Heat to near smoking. Place filled cucumber logs, meat side down, into hot oil. Cook over medium-high to high heat until meat is lightly browned.

(2) Add broth. Bring to boil. Scatter carrots slices, cloud ears and tiger lily flowers on top of cucumber. Cover and simmer 15 - 20 minutes or until cucumber is soft and filling is thoroughly cooked. (Up to this point can be done the day before. Simmer about 10 minutes to reheat then proceed to the next step.)

CUCUMBER LOGS (continued)

(3) Remove cucumber logs with a slotted spoon. Arrange, meat side up, on a preheated serving platter. Garnish with carrot slices, cloud ears and tiger lily flowers.

(4) Thicken pan gravy with cornstarch mixture. Add salt to taste and spoon over finished dish.

KITCHEN HINT: Have a supply of yellowed (over matured) cucumbers in your garden? Do not discard. Use in this or other cucumber recipes.

KITCHEN HINT: Make small meatballs with any leftover meat mixture. Add to frying pan during step (2) and cook with cucumber logs.

****

Practical Variations

SUMMER SQUASH BOATS
Substitute: *1 - 2 zucchini* and *1 - 2 yellow squash* for the *cucumbers* Cut lengthwise. Scoop out and discard seeds. Fill hollowed out squash with meat mixture.

Add: *1 tablespoon regular soy sauce* to cornstarch mixture
          ¼ teaspoon Asian chili sauce to cornstarch mixture

BITTER MELON LOGS
Substitute: *3 - 5 long bitter melons* for the *cucumbers*

Add: *1 tablespoon oyster sauce* to the cornstarch mixture
          ¼ teaspoon ground white or *black pepper or to taste*

STUFFED PEPPERS
Substitute: *Red peppers, green peppers, yellow peppers* and/or *jalapeño peppers* for the *cucumbers*.

❶ Cut red, green and yellow peppers in half, lengthwise. Remove and discard seeds and membranes. Cut each half into about 1½ - 2-inch square pieces. Mound with about 1 tablespoon meat mixture.

❷ Cut a small piece from stem end of jalapeño. Scoop out and discard seeds and membrane. Fill cavity with meat mixture.

OR cut jalapeños in half lengthwise, remove and discard membrane and seeds. Fill with meat mixture.

STEAMED PORK PEARL BALLS

serves 4 - 5

1 cup glutinous rice Soak 2 - 3 hours. Drain well just before using

1 pound lean ground pork	)
3 Chinese dried mushrooms (1½" diameter) Soak	)
in water at least ½ hour to soften. Remove	)
and discard stems. Finely chop caps.	) Combine well.
2 tablespoons finely chopped water chestnuts	) Can be done
1 small onion Finely chopped	) up to the day
1 egg Lightly beaten	) before and
1½ teaspoons kosher salt or to taste	) refrigerated.
¼ teaspoon sugar	)
dash of white or *black pepper or to taste*	)
1 tablespoon ginger wine, p. 16	)
1 tablespoon regular soy sauce	)

¼ - 1 teaspoon Asian chili sauce (optional)	) Combine in a small
2 tablespoons regular soy sauce	) serving bowl.
1 - 2 tablespoons rice vinegar	) This is the sauce.

1 - 2 pounds napa cabbage Thinly sliced.

(1) Add water in steamer base. Place steamer basket or steamer rack on steamer base and line with napa cabbage. Steam, covered, until cabbage is wilted.

(2) Gently shape meat mixture into balls, using about 1 tablespoon mixture. Roll into drained rice to coat completely. Arrange on wilted cabbage.

(3) Steam, covered, over high heat for 30 minutes. Serve hot with sauce.
****

Practical Variations

STEAMED TURKEY PEARL BALLS
Substitute: *1 pound ground turkey* for the *ground pork*

PORK & SHRIMP PEARL BALLS
Substitute: *6 ounces raw shrimp* for *4 ounces ground pork* Shell and devein shrimp. Minced or coarsely chopped.

HONEY TANGERINE PORK CHOPS

serves 3 - 5

2 - 2½ pounds (about 5) ¾-inch thick pork chops

Thumb-size piece of ginger Peeled. Crushed.	) Combine.
1 teaspoon kosher salt or to taste	) Add pork chops and
1 tablespoon dark or ***mushroom soy sauce***	) coat each one well.
1 tablespoon oil	) Marinate 2 hours or
¾ cup honey tangerine juice	) overnight in the
or ***other sweet citrus juice***	) refrigerator.

2 - 3 tablespoons honey or as needed for basting
1 tablespoon finely shredded fresh tangerine zest free of white membrane
2 - 4 cloves garlic Finely shredded or thinly sliced.
1 scallion Shredded or thinly sliced.
1 - 2 tablespoons oil
ginger and *marinade from pork chops*

¾ teaspoon cornstarch	) Combine in a small bowl.
1 tablespoon water	) Stir well just before adding to saucepan.

(1) Place an oven rack in middle of oven. Preheat oven on to 450°.

(2) Drain pork chops. Place on lightly oiled broiler grid or on a rack set over roasting pan. Brush with honey. Bake in middle of oven for 15 minutes.

(3) Turn chops. Brush with honey. Add ¼ cup hot water to bottom of baking pan. Bake another 14 - 20 minutes or until reached desired doneness.

(4) While chops are baking, heat a small saucepan. Add oil, tangerine zest, garlic and scallion. Stir-fry over medium heat until tangerine zest is fragrant, about 3 - 4 minutes. Add marinade, including ginger. Bring to boil. Simmer 5 minutes. Thicken with cornstarch mixture.

(5) Arrange pork chops on serving platter. Remove and discard ginger. Spoon sauce on top. Serve. Garnish with parsley, if desired.

Alternative cooking method: Broil pork chops, in middle of oven, 6 - 7 minutes or until nicely browned. Turn, broil 6 - 8 minutes or until pork chops reach desired doneness.

KITCHEN HINT: For sweeter chops, brush each side with honey twice.
KITCHEN HINT: To crush ginger, place chunk of ginger on cutting board. Place wide side of knife or cleaver on top of ginger. Hit the knife or cleaver with a fist or the heel of your palm.
KITCHEN HINT: Use the back of a paring knife or a teaspoon to scrape off the white membrane from tangerine zest.

STIR-FRY HAM & ASPARAGUS

serves 3 - 5

12 ounces cooked ham (*one thick slice*) Cut into about 1½x½x½-inch logs.

1 pound fresh asparagus Peel root end. Remove scales if needed, p. 99.
   Slant-cut into about ½-inch thick slices.

1 large onion Peeled. Cut in half lengthwise. Slice the halves thinly.

2 - 3 cloves garlic Minced

½ teaspoon kosher salt or to taste

Dash of white pepper or to taste

2 - 3 tablespoons oil

½ cup chicken broth or ***water***

1 teaspoon cornstarch) Combine in a small bowl.	
1 tablespoon water) Stir well just before adding to wok.	

(1) Heat wok. Add oil. Swirl to coat wok. Add onion and garlic. Stir-fry over
   medium-high heat for about 1 minute.

(2) Add salt and asparagus. Stir-fry over high heat until asparagus changes color,
   about 2 - 3 minutes.

(3) Stir in ham and white pepper. Add broth. Cover. Bring to a boil. Thicken
   with cornstarch mixture. Serve hot.

****

Practical Variations

STIR-FRY HAM & MIXED VEGETABLES

Substitute: ***1 pound any assorted vegetables*** or ***frozen mixed vegetables***
            for the ***asparagus***

Add: ***Minced fresh chili*** or ***Asian chili sauce to taste*** during step (1)
            ½ - 1 teaspoon Asian sesame oil during step (3)

KITCHEN HINT: If time permits, thaw and drain frozen vegetables before stir-frying.

STIR-FRY PRECOOKED MEAT & 3 PEPPERS

Substitute: ***12 ounces any kind of precooked meat*** for the ***ham***
            1 each red, yellow and ***green pepper*** for the ***asparagus*** Remove
            and discard seeds and membranes. Cut into thin strips.

Add: ***1 tablespoon oyster sauce*** or ***regular soy sauce*** to ***cornstarch
            mixture***

SEAFOOD

SEAFOOD RECIPES IN OTHER SECTIONS OF THIS BOOK

STIR-FRY SESAME PERCH CUBES

serves 3 - 4

1 pound perch fillet Cut into about 1-inch cubes	)
¾ teaspoon kosher salt or to taste	) Combine well.
1 teaspoon sugar	) Marinate ½ hour
1 tablespoon ginger wine, p. 16	) but no more than
4 slices ginger from ginger wine, p. 16	) 1 hour in the
1 tablespoon regular soy sauce	) refrigerator.
1 tablespoon sesame oil or to taste	)

1 tablespoon toasted black sesame seeds (optional)
1 large Spanish or vidalia onion Cut into about 1½-inch chunks
½ cup chicken broth
2 - 3 tablespoons oil

1 teaspoon cornstarch	) Combine in a small bowl.
1 tablespoon water	) Stir well just before adding to wok.

(1) Heat a wok. Add oil. Swirl to coat wok. Heat to smoking. Add perch cubes. Stir-fry, gently, over high heat until nearly done, 3 - 4 minutes. Remove to a plate, leaving oil in wok.

(2) Add onion to wok. Stir-fry over high heat 1 - 2 minutes or just under the way you like your onion. Add fish and broth. Cover and bring to a boil, simmer 1 - 2 minutes or until perch is just cooked. Thicken with cornstarch mixture. Remove to a serving platter. Sprinkle sesame seeds on top. Serve hot.

****

Practical Variation

STIR-FRY PERCH CUBES WITH FRESH CHILIES
Add: *1 - 3 fresh green or red chili peppers* Discard membrane and seeds. Cut into thin strips. Add to wok at the same time as onion.

STIR-FRY SALMON CUBES
Substitute: *1 pound salmon fillet* for the *perch fillet*

KITCHEN HINT: Cook the fish with the skin on. This will ensure that the cubes do not fall apart.
KITCHEN HINT: When toasting black sesame seeds, add a few white ones. When the white sesame seeds are toasted, the black ones are toasted also.

SWEET & SOUR FISH

1 pound flounder fillet Cut into about 2 x 3-inch pieces or leave whole.	)
1 tablespoon ginger wine, p. 16	) Combine and mix well.) Do not marinate more than
1 tablespoon regular soy sauce	) 1 hour in the refrigerator.
1 egg white Lightly beaten	)

¼ cup all purpose flour	) Combine on a piece of wax paper or on a
¼ cup cornstarch	) plate. This is the coating for the fish.

½ - 1 carrot Peeled. Shredded finely.

½ - 1 medium onion Peeled. Sliced thinly.

3 - 5 Chinese dried mushrooms Soak in water at least ½ hour to soften. Squeeze out excess water. Remove and discard stems. Slice caps thinly.

½ green pepper Remove and discard seeds and membrane. Sliced thinly.

oil for pan frying

1 teaspoon kosher salt or to taste	)
2 tablespoons sugar	)
2 tablespoons regular soy sauce	) Combine in a bowl.
2 tablespoons ketchup	) This is the sauce.
3 tablespoons white vinegar	)
¾ cup water	)

1 tablespoon cornstarch	) Combine in a small bowl.
2 tablespoons water	) Stir well just before adding to pan.

(1) Coat fish with flour mixture. Shake off excess.

(2) Pour about ¼-inch oil in a frying pan. Heat until near smoking. Pan fry fish slices until browned on both sides. Remove. Drain on paper towels. Arrange on warm serving platter.

(3) Discard oil and crumbs in frying pan. Wipe clean and return to range.

(4) Add 1 - 2 tablespoons oil to frying pan. Add carrot, onion and mushrooms. Stir-fry over high heat about 1 minute. Add sauce. Bring to boil. Thicken with cornstarch mixture. Stir in green pepper. Spoon over fried fish. Serve.

KITCHEN HINT: Fish browns very quickly. Have everything ready and within easy reach before beginning to pan fry.

KITCHEN HINT: Any non-oily, light-flavor fish can be substituted for the flounder.

SHRIMP IN BLACK BEAN SAUCE serves 3 - 4

1 pound raw shrimp Shelled. Deveined.) Toss well. Let stand 15
    Washed and pat dry with paper towels.) minutes. Can be done the
¾ teaspoon kosher salt   ) day before. Refrigerated.

4 ounces lean ground pork
1 tablespoon fermented black beans Rinsed and drained
1 - 2 cloves garlic Minced
½ teaspoon sugar
dash white pepper or to taste
1 tablespoon ginger wine, p. 16
1 teaspoon regular soy sauce
1 scallion Cleaned and thinly sliced. Reserve 1 tablespoon.
3 - 4 tablespoons oil
¾ cup chicken broth
2 eggs Lightly beaten

1 tablespoon cornstarch) Combine in a small bowl.
2 tablespoons water   ) Stir well just before adding to wok.

(1) Heat wok or frying pan. Add 2 - 3 tablespoons oil. Swirl to coat wok. Heat until near smoking. Add shrimp. Stir-fry over high heat until shrimp changes color. Remove to a plate.

(2) Add 1 tablespoon oil to wok. Add fermented black beans and garlic. Stir-fry over medium-high heat until fragrant, 1 - 2 minutes. Add pork. Stir-fry until pork changes color. Stir in sugar, white pepper, ginger wine, soy sauce and scallion. Mix thoroughly. Add shrimp and mix well. Add broth. Cover. Bring to a boil. Simmer until shrimp is cooked.

(3) Thicken with cornstarch mixture. Slowly stir in beaten eggs. Remove to a serving platter as soon as eggs are cooked. Sprinkle reserved scallion on top. Serve at once.

NOTE: This is the famous **Shrimp in Lobster Sauce** sans lobster.

CORAL SHRIMP VARIATION

1 pound large raw shrimp Shelled) Deveined. Washed and pat dry.) **½ teaspoon kosher salt**)	Combine. Marinate at least ½ hour. Can be done the day before and refrigerated.

4 tablespoons oil
4 slices fresh ginger
2 scallions Cleaned and sliced thinly
2 - 4 cloves garlic Minced

1 tablespoon ginger wine, p. 16) **3 tablespoons ketchup**) **2 tablespoons broth** or **water**) **1 teaspoon sugar**)	Combine in a small bowl. This is the sauce.

(1) Heat wok. Add oil. Swirl to coat wok. Add ginger slices. Heat on high until oil reaches smoking point. Add shrimp. Stir-fry over high heat until color changes. Remove shrimp to a plate. Remove and discard ginger slices.

(2) Remove all but 1 tablespoon oil from wok. Add scallion and garlic. Stir-fry until fragrant, about 1 - 2 minutes. Stir in sauce. Add precooked shrimp, stir-fry until shrimp is cooked and coated with sauce. Serve at once.

****

Practical Variation

CORAL FISH

Substitute: ¾ **pound fish fillet** for the **shrimp** Cut fish into bite-size pieces.
Add: ¼ **cup frozen green peas** Thawed and drained. Add at the same time as shrimp during step (2).
             1 - 2 tablespoons chopped Chinese parsley Sprinkle on finished dish.

SHRIMP, NUTS & VEGETABLES

serves 3 - 4

---

1 pound large or medium raw shrimp Shelled.) Toss together
    Deveined. Washed and pat dry. Split in half   ) shrimp and salt.
    lengthwise or cut into 2 or 3 crosswise pieces.) Let stand 15
½ - ¾ teaspoon kosher salt   ) minutes.

---

1 - 2 scallions Cleaned. Smash white part. Cut whole scallion into 2-inch
    lengths.

3 slices ginger from ginger wine, p. 16

1 - 2 dried or fresh chili peppers (optional) Finely chopped.

1 - 3 cloves garlic Minced

1½ tablespoons ginger wine, p. 16

1 teaspoon sugar

1 small Spanish onion Peeled and diced (about the size of peas)

1 cup frozen peas & carrots Thawed

½ cup diced (size of peas) bamboo shoots

2 teaspoons kosher salt or to taste

½ - ¾ cup chicken broth or water

3 - 4 tablespoons oil

1 cup toasted nuts (peanuts, cashews or *almonds)*

---

2 teaspoons cornstarch) Combine in a small bowl.
1 tablespoon water   ) Stir well just before adding to wok.

---

(1) Heat wok. Add 3 tablespoons oil. Swirl to coat wok. Add ginger and
    scallions. Stir-fry over high heat until ginger slices turn brown. Remove and
    discard both the ginger and scallions.

(2) Add chili and garlic. Stir-fry a few seconds. Add shrimp. Stir-fry over high
    heat until color changes. Add ginger wine and sugar. Mix well. Remove to a
    plate.

(3) Add 1 tablespoon oil to wok, if needed. Add salt, onion, peas & carrots and
    bamboo shoots. Stir-fry 2 minutes. Add broth. Cover. Bring to a boil. Boil 1
    minute. Add shrimp. Mix well. Thicken with cornstarch mixture. Stir in nuts
    and serve at once.

KITCHEN HINT: Splitting the shrimp lengthwise is more time consuming, but the cooked shrimp
        look and taste better and so makes the extra effort worthwhile. This step can be
        done ahead of time.

SPICY SHRIMP, SNOW PEAS & BABY CORN
serves 3 - 4

1 pound raw shrimp Shelled. Deveined. Washed and pat dry.

¼ - 2 teaspoons Asian chili sauce)	Combine. Add shrimp. Mix
½ teaspoon kosher salt)	well. Let stand 15 minutes. Can
1 teaspoon sugar)	be done day before. Refrigerated.

1 scallion Cleaned and sliced thinly

3 slices fresh ginger Minced

2 - 3 cloves garlic Minced

1 tablespoon ginger wine, p. 16

6 ounces snow peas Stringed

1 can baby corn Rinsed and drained. Leave whole or cut in halves.

1 onion Cut into small wedges.

Few strips red pepper

¾ teaspoon kosher salt or to taste

3 - 4 tablespoons oil

¼ - ½ cup chicken broth

1 teaspoon cornstarch)	Combine in a small bowl.
1 tablespoon water)	Stir well just before adding to wok.

(1) Heat wok. Add 2 - 3 tablespoons oil. Swirl to coat wok. Add scallion, ginger and garlic. Stir-fry over high heat until fragrant, about 1 minute. Add shrimp. Stir-fry over high heat until shrimp change color. Add ginger wine. Mix well. Remove to a plate and set aside.

(2) Add 1 tablespoon oil to wok. Add salt, snow peas, baby corn and onion. Stir-fry until snow peas change color. Add broth. Cover. Boil 1 minute.

(3) Add shrimp and red pepper. Stir-fry until shrimp is cooked. Thicken with cornstarch mixture. Serve at once.

SHRIMP WITH STRAW MUSHROOMS
Serves 3 - 4

1 pound raw shrimp Shelled. Deveined.	)
Washed and pat dry.	) Combine. Marinate 15
¾ teaspoon kosher salt	) minutes. Can be done the
1 teaspoon sugar	) day before. Refrigerated.
dash white pepper or to taste	)

1 scallion Cleaned. Cut both green and white into 1-inch lengths.

3 slices fresh ginger

2 - 3 cloves garlic Smashed.

1 tablespoon ginger wine, p. 16

1 carrot Peeled. Slant cut into thin slices.

1 can straw mushrooms, peeled or *unpeeled* Rinsed. Drained.

1 8-ounce can sliced water chestnuts

½ - 1 small green pepper Cut into about 1-inch squares.

3 - 4 tablespoons oil

½ cup chicken broth or *water*	)
1 tablespoon oyster sauce or to taste	) Combine in a small bowl.
ground white or *black pepper to taste*	) This is the sauce.
½ teaspoon sugar	)

2 teaspoons cornstarch	) Combine in a small bowl.
1 tablespoon water	) Stir well just before adding to wok.

(1) Heat wok. Add 2 - 3 tablespoons oil. Swirl to coat wok. Add scallion, ginger and garlic. Stir-fry over high heat until garlic begins to brown. Remove and discard all three. Add shrimp. Stir-fry over high heat until color changes. Stir in wine. Remove to a plate and set aside.

(2) Add 1 tablespoon oil to wok, if needed, add carrot, stir-fry over high heat about 30 seconds. Add straw mushrooms and water chestnuts, stir-fry another 2 minutes. Stir in shrimp and green pepper. Add sauce. Cover. Bring to a boil. Thicken with cornstarch mixture. Serve at once.

****

Practical Variations

SHRIMP WITH PORTABELLA MUSHROOMS

Substitute: *8 - 12 ounces portabella mushroom*s for the *straw mushrooms*
Slice portabella mushrooms into about ½-inch thick slices.

SNOW PEAS SCALLOPS

serves 3 - 4

1 pound sea scallops Washed and pat dry. Cut across into 2 or 3 disks.

1 teaspoon ginger wine, p. 16	) Combine.
1 teaspoon cornstarch	) Add scallops. Toss well.
½ teaspoon kosher salt or to taste	) Marinate ½ hour or over-
dash of white pepper or to taste	) night in the refrigerator.

¾ pound snow peas Stringed
1 onion Peeled and thinly sliced
4 slices ginger from ginger wine, p. 16
2 - 4 cloves garlic Crushed
1 teaspoon kosher salt or to taste
½ teaspoon sugar
½ cup chicken broth
3 - 4 tablespoons oil

2 teaspoons cornstarch	) Combine in a small bowl.
1 tablespoon water	) Stir well just before adding to wok.

(1) Heat wok. Add 1 - 2 tablespoons oil. Swirl to coat wok. Add salt, onion and snow peas. Stir-fry over high heat until snow peas change color, adding broth 1 tablespoon at a time if wok seems dry. Remove to a plate.

(2) Add 2 tablespoons oil to wok. Add ginger and garlic. Stir-fry over medium high heat until garlic begins to brown. Remove and discard both. Add scallops. Stir-fry gently over high heat until color changes, about 2 minutes. Stir in vegetables, broth and sugar. Bring to boil. Cover and simmer 1 - 2 minutes. Thicken with cornstarch mixture. Serve at once.

****

Practical Variations

SNOW PEAS CHICKEN

Substitute: ***1 pound boneless and skinless chicken breast*** for the ***scallops*** Cut chicken into about ¼-inch thick slices.

Add: ***1 tablespoon regular soy sauce*** to marinade.

SNOW PEAS TOFU

Substitute: ***1 pound firm tofu*** for the ***scallops*** Cut tofu into about ¼-inch thick slices.

Add: ***1 tablespoon dark or mushroom soy sauce*** to marinade.

SEA SCALLOPS WITH FRESH CHINESE MUSHROOMS & CUCUMBER

serves 3 - 4

1 pound sea scallops Washed and pat dry. Cut across into 2 or 3 disks.

1 teaspoon ginger juice or to taste	)
1 teaspoon cornstarch	) Combine. Add scallops. Toss
½ teaspoon kosher salt or to taste	) well. Marinate ½ hour.
¼ teaspoon sugar	)

1 - 3 cloves garlic Minced

4 - 6 ounces fresh Chinese mushrooms Remove stems. Slice and use tender parts. Discard hard woody parts. Cut caps into about ½-inch thick slices.

½ - 1 small carrot Peeled and sliced thinly.

1 cucumber Peeled. Cut in half lengthwise. Remove and discard seeds. Cut into about ½-inch thick slices.

1 - 2 scallions Cleaned. Shredded or sliced thinly

3 - 4 tablespoons oil

2 teaspoons cornstarch	)
¼ cup chicken broth	) Combine in a small bowl. Stir
½ teaspoon kosher salt or to taste	) well just before adding to wok.
1 tablespoon oyster sauce	)

(1) Heat wok or frying pan. Add 1 - 2 tablespoons oil. Add garlic, carrot and mushrooms. Stir-fry over medium high heat until mushrooms are limp. Add cucumber and scallions. Stir-fry over high heat until cucumber is heated through. Remove to a plate and set aside.

(2) Add 2 tablespoons oil to wok. Heat until near smoking. Add scallops. Stir-fry gently over high heat until color changes to white, about 2 minutes.

(3) Add vegetables. Stir-fry, gently, until scallops are cooked, 1 - 2 minutes. Stir in broth mixture. Bring to a boil. Mix well. Serve at once.

****

Practical Variations

CHICKEN WITH FRESH CHINESE MUSHROOMS & CUCUMBERS

Substitute: *1 pound boneless* and *skinless chicken breast* for the *scallops*

Add: *¼ - 1 teaspoon Asian chili sauce* during step (2)

SEEDS & NUTS

ROASTING

Nothing can compare with the crisp, full flavor and aroma of freshly roasted seeds and nuts. Roasting seeds and nuts at home is really easy, they are tastier that the store bought ones and more importantly you can control the salt content. To roast a small quantity of shelled seeds or nuts:

(1) Place shelled seeds or nuts in an unoiled wok or frying pan.
(2) Cook, using medium-low to medium heat, until golden, stirring frequently, 4 - 7 minutes depending on the kind of seeds or nuts.
(3) Immediately transfer roasted seeds or nuts to a clean plate to cool.

To roast a larger quantity, simply spread shelled seeds or nuts on baking sheet. Bake in a 300° preheated oven, stirring once or twice, until you are surrounded with a deliciously nutty aroma, check frequently as soon as nuts start to color.

Almonds	16 - 20 minutes	Pine nuts	8 - 10 minutes
Cashews	15 - 17 minutes	Sesame seeds	4 - 6 minutes
Peanuts	12 - 15 minutes	Sunflower seeds	25 - 35 minutes
Pecans	18 - 22 minutes	Walnuts	26 - 30 minutes

BLANCHING

Cover shelled nuts with boiling water. Let stand 10 - 15 minutes. Slip off skin.

DEEP FRYING

(1) In a 2- to 3- quart pot, heat about 2 inches of oil to about 365°.
(2) Add 1 cup shelled nuts and deep fry until lightly golden.
(3) Remove and drain on paper towels.

KITCHEN HINT: When roasting black sesame seeds, add a few white ones to act as control. When the white sesame seeds are golden, the black ones are roasted.

KITCHEN HINT: To maintain the quality of seeds and nuts, place them in a freezer bag or freezer container, date, label and freeze. Will keep up to 2 years.

****

ROASTING CHESTNUTS IN A WOK

1 pound fresh chestnuts
2 teaspoons oil

(1) Place wok on range. Turn range to low. While wok is heating, using a sharp small knife, cut a cross-shape through the flat side of the chestnut shells.
(3) Turn range to medium. Add chestnuts and oil to wok. Stir to coat chestnuts.
(4) Cover wok. Roast chestnuts for 15 - 18 minutes or until chestnuts are roasted, shaking wok every 5 minutes. Serve hot.

CHINESE PASTRIES, COOKIES & FRUITS

My students enjoyed the various pastries, cookies and fruits that I introduced to them during our cooking classes. They felt that I should incorporate these in my cookbook.

The following are some of the pastries available in a typical Chinese cake shop.

MOON CAKES: Made in carved wooden moon cake molds, moon cakes can be round or square, about 3 inches across and about 1¼ inches thick. These cakes, baked to a rich brown color, are sweet and very rich.
The filling, wrapped with a thin cake-like dough, can be of lotus seed paste, black bean paste or mixed nuts. Sold with or without salted egg yolk (1, 2 or 3) in the center (the 3 yolks being the most expensive).
Can be purchased single or in box of four. Cut into small wedges to serve. Moon cakes freeze well. Thaw and bring to room temperature before serving.

MELON CAKES: These are white, round, about 3-inch diameter, semi-flaky pastry, filled with sweetened wintermelon.
Can be purchased single or in roll of five. Cut into quarters to serve. Melon cake freezes well. Thaw and bring to room temperature before serving.

LOTUS SEED CAKES: Same as melon cakes but with sweet lotus seed paste filling. Lotus seed cake freezes well. Thaw and bring to room temperature before serving.

BLACK BEAN CAKES: Same as melon cakes but with sweet black bean paste filling. Black bean cake freezes well. Thaw and bring to room temperature before serving.

NOODLE CAKES: Made with fried noodles, honey and walnuts. A bit sticky but delicious. Noodle cake freezes well. Thaw and bring to room temperature before serving.

EGG CUSTARD: A semi-flaky tartlet filled with sweet egg custard. Can be served at room temperature, but much nicer when served warm. Heat at 300° for about 10 minutes. Egg custard freezes well. Reheat thawed or frozen.

CHINESE PASTRIES, COOKIES & FRUITS (continued)

SESAME RICE DUMPLINGS (BALLS):	Large balls made from glutinous rice flour, coated with sesame seeds, filled with black bean paste and deep fried to a rich golden brown.
SPONGE CAKE, WHITE:	Made with rice flour and sugar. This sponge cake is steamed Serve cold or hot (by steaming).
SPONGE CAKE, BROWN:	Same as white sponge cake but made with brown sugar instead of white sugar.
STEAMED SPONGE CAKE:	Made with flour, sugar and eggs. This sponge cake is steamed instead of baked. Serve cold or hot (by steaming).

The following cookies are available in most Asian markets.

FUN WON (PHOENIX) ROLLS:	A very light and delicate cookie. Made with flour, egg and sugar.
COCONUT ROLLS:	Look like miniature cake rolls. These cookies are made with flour, sugar, coconut and eggs.
ALMOND COOKIES:	These little round cookies, made in carved wooden molds, are made with flour, almond powder and sugar. There are many different versions. Try different brands to find the one you like best.

The following canned fruits are available in Chinese grocery stores. The fresh fruits, when in season, are also available at fruits stands in Chinatown and some local supermarkets.

LICHEE:	Also spelled litchi and lychee. A tropical fruit. The fresh fruit is about the size and shape of a large strawberry. Peel and discard the thin, bumpy, red skin to reveal the white, soft, juicy pulp that is deliciously sweet with a flavor of its own. In the center is a black seed which is not edible. Fresh lichee is available during the summer months. Canned lichee is fresh lichee, peeled, seeded and packed in heavy syrup.

To Serve: * Chilled and serve alone
                 * Use as a garnish for ice cream
                 * Mixed with fresh melon balls
                 * Combined with other canned fruits

Dried lichee does not look or taste like fresh lichee. Under the dried browned skin is a raisiny-pulp that is sweet and a bit chewy. Taste like a cross between a raisin and a date.

LONGAN: Literal translation means dragon eye. The name was given because of the big black shiny seed in the center of the fresh fruit.

Longan is a tropical fruit about the size of a large marble. Peel and discard the thin, light-brown skin to reveal the translucent, gray-white, juicy pulp that has a delicate sweet taste. The large black seed in the center is not edible. Fresh longan is available during the summer months.

Canned longan is fresh longan, peeled, seeded and packed in heavy syrup. It maintains the delicate flavor of the fresh fruit.

To serve: * Chilled and serve alone
                * Combined with other fresh fruits
                * Combined with berries

Dried longan still looks like the fresh fruit on the outside. The pulp, however, is brown, sweet, chewy and a bit smoky.

LOQUAT: A golden color fruit that resembles an apricot in size and color.

Canned loquat is packed in heavy syrup.

To serve: * Chilled and serve alone
                * Use as garnish for ice cream
                * Combine with other fruits.

COLLECTION OF KITCHEN HINTS

☺ Raw meat, raw poultry, raw seafood or raw eggs - For ease of cleaning, rinse away any residues from kitchen tools and equipment with cold or lukewarm water before washing with hot water or placing in the dishwasher.

☺ Rust on carbon steel, spun steel or cast iron wok - Wipe rust areas with vinegar, wait a few seconds and watch the rust disappear. Repeat if necessary. Wash wok with soap and water, dry thoroughly and season (read Woks, p. 7).

☺ Cover burnt pot with undiluted vinegar. Let soak for 2 hours, overnight for stubborn burns. Burnt on food will lift right off. Repeat if necessary.

☺ Removing garlic smell from fingers - Rub a piece of stainless steel flatware between fingers (or rub your fingers on the stainless sink) under cold running water. Garlic smell will disappear.

☺ Removing seafood smell from hands - Rub with vinegar followed by washing with soap and water.

☺ To prevent insects from attacking dried ingredients like rice, beans, lotus roots, mushrooms, pasta, etc. Place dried ingredients together with a few bay leaves in a container with a tight fitting lid (I prefer a glass container).

☺ Use an egg slicer to slice button mushrooms. Also great for slicing cooked potatoes for potato salad

☺ Keeping herbs fresh - Trim stems, place trimmed herbs in a glass ⅓ filled with water, cover loosely with a plastic bag that have the two corners cut away. Keep in the refrigerator.

☺ Removing fat from broth or stew - Place a piece of plastic wrap on the surface of the broth, the fat will stick to the plastic wrap. Discard fat-coated plastic wrap, repeat if necessary.

☺ Rehydrating dried ingredients - Place ingredients in a deep container that will allow ingredients to be completely submerged and have sufficient room for expansion when filled ⅔ with water. Place a piece of plastic wrap (a few inches larger than the container) on the water surface. Pour additional water on top of the plastic wrap to fill container. Dried ingredients will remain fully submerged.

☺ Ketchup won't flow - Insert a chopstick to the bottom of the bottle of ketchup then remove. Ketchup will now flow freely.

☺ Cleaning copper - Sprinkle salt on wet copper surface, rub with a slice of lemon. Repeat if necessary. Wash and dry.

COLLECTION OF KITCHEN HINTS (continued)

☺ Eating on the run - Roll stir-fry in a soft tortilla or fill in pita halves.

☺ Soy sauce stain on fabric - Saturate stained area with hair spray, let stand 15 - 30 minutes launder as usual (works for ball-point ink stains, too.) Or saturate stained area with full-strength liquid laundry detergent.

☺ Cleaning stainless steel kitchenware - Rub with undiluted white vinegar.

☺ Freeze leftover coffee and tea in ice cube trays. Once frozen, remove to freezer bag, date, label and freeze. Use in iced coffee and iced tea.

☺ Sauce too thin - Slowly stir in a mixture of 1 part cornstarch (or potato starch or tapioca starch) to 2 parts of water until proper consistency is reached.

☺ Sauce too thick - Stir in warm liquid until proper consistency is reached.

☺ Too much salt - Cook an accompanying dish without salt. Eaten together one will balance out the other.

☺ Frequently used vegetables - Wash, peel and cut extra. Place in a plastic bag with a paper towel. Refrigerate.

☺ To save time, if practical, set aside a block of time to ready ingredients for multiple meals. I like to set aside a morning to wash, and maybe cut, vegetables, slice and marinate meats and poultry for 2 - 3 days' meals.

☺ When making changes to a recipe, write the initial changes in pencil. After a second testing turns out satisfactory, rewrite the changes in ink.

☺ Rub a bit of nail polish remover on the hard-to-remove pricetags and stickers on glass, cookwares, etc. Allow to soak 5 - 10 minutes then peel.

☺ Wilted and tired-looking vegetables - Soak in cold water to freshen.

☺ Place a damp kitchen towel or a damp paper towel under cutting board to prevent it from moving when in use.

☺ Place a damp napkin under a dish on a tray to prevent it from moving.

☺ Place zipper bag filled with a few ice cubes in freezer before going on vacation. If there is one solid chunk of ice in the bag when you return, there was a power failure while you were away and items in your freezer have thawed.

☺ Look for additional kitchen hints throughout this book.

☺ Look for additional kitchen hints, do-ahead information and time-saving tips in my cookbook *Wokking Your Way to Low Cooking*.

LIST OF INGREDIENTS IN ENGLISH & CHINESE

Due to the many dialects of Chinese, an ingredient, because of different regional pronunciations, can end up with different spellings when translated into English. To further complicate matters, different manufacturers will frequently use different English for the same ingredient. Then there is mistranslation. An example is "Red Bean Curd." On the bottle of one manufacturer's label the English reads "Bean Sauce" but the Chinese reads "Red Bean Curd." Not to mention the fact that red bean curd and bean sauce are two entirely different ingredients. The following list has helped my students (those who do not read Chinese) in their shopping expeditions. I hope it will help you, too. Make a copy of the list and bring it with you whenever you go shopping for Chinese ingredients.

Adzuki beans 紅豆

Almond cookies 杏仁餅

Angled luffa 絲瓜

Baby corn 玉米筍

Bamboo shoots, chunk 竹筍

　　　　　shredded 筍絲

　　　　　tip 筍尖

Bean sauce 原晒豉

Bean sprouts, mung 芽菜仔

　　　　　soy 大豆芽菜

Bean threads 粉絲

Bitter melon 苦瓜

Black bean cake 豆沙酥

Bok choy 白菜

Bull Head barbecue sauce 沙茶醬

Chili oil 辣油

Chili sauce 辣椒醬

Chinese chives 韮菜

Chinese eggplant 茄子, 矮瓜

Chinese long beans 豆角, 長江豆

Chinese mushrooms 冬菇

Chinese noodles 麵

Chinese pancake 薄餅

Chinese parsley 芫茜, 香菜

Chinese radish 蘿蔔

Chinese red dates 紅棗

Chinese roast pork 义燒

Chinese rock sugar 冰糖

Chinese sausage 臘腸

Choy sum 菜心

Cloud ears 雲耳

Coconut rolls 椰子蛋捲

Creamy-Chinese style dried noodles 奶油麵

Curry powder 咖喱粉

Dried bean curd 腐竹

Dried chili peppers 乾辣椒

Dried scallops 干貝, 干瑤柱

Egg custard 蛋撻

Fermented bean curd 白腐乳

Fermented black beans 豆豉

Fish sauce 魚露

Five-spice powder 五香粉

Fuzzy melon 節瓜 毛瓜

Gai lan 芥蘭

Gingko nuts 白果

Green soy beans 毛豆

Ho fun	沙河粉	Sesame paste	芝蔴醬
Hoisin sauce	海鮮醬	Sesame seeds, black	黑芝蔴
Hong Kong style pan fried noodles	港式炒麵	white	白芝蔴
Ja choy	搾菜	Shanghai bok choy	上海白菜
Laver	紫菜	Sichuan peppercorns	花椒
Lichee	荔枝	Soy sauce, dark	老抽
Longan	龍眼	mushroom	草菰老抽
Loquat	枇杷果	regular	生抽
Lotus root, dried	藕片乾	Sponge cake, brown	黃糖糕
fresh	蓮藕	white	白糖糕
Lotus seed cake	蓮蓉酥	Spring roll skin	春捲皮
Melon cake	老婆餅	Star anise	八角
Moon cake	月餅	Straw mushrooms	草菇
Napa cabbage	黃芽白	Tapioca starch	菱粉
Noodle cake	西騎馬	Taro root	芋頭
Ong choi	空心菜	Tianjin bean sheets	天津粉皮
Oyster sauce	蠔油	Tiger lily flowers	金針菜
Preserved eggs	皮蛋	Tofu	豆腐
Preserved plums	酸梅	Tofu, deep fried	油豆腐
Red bean curd	南乳	5-spiced pressed	上海五香干
Rice, brown	糙米	Vinegar, Chinese red	浙醋
glutinous	糯米	Chinkiang	鎮江香醋
jasmine	香米	rice	白米醋
Rice cake	年糕片, 白粿片	Water chestnuts	馬蹄
Rice sticks	米粉, 挑粉	Wintermelon	冬瓜
Sesame oil	蔴油	Wonton wrappers	雲吞皮

My Students' Favorite Chinese Recipes, updated edition

GLOSSARY OF INGREDIENTS

ADZUKI BEANS: *Description:* Small dried, dark red beans with a white ridge along one side. *Storage:* Room temperature. *Preparation:* Cook and use as you would any dry beans. In Asian cuisine, it is made into a sweet soup that is served hot or cold as a snack or dessert. Also used to make popsicle and ice cream. Sweetened, pureed beans, known as red bean paste or black bean paste, is the filling in black bean cake, moon cake and other pastries. Prepared bean paste are sold in cans at Asian markets. *Availability:* Always. Asian markets in 1 pound plastic bags and health food stores.

ALMOND COOKIES: See page 167.

ANGLED LUFFA: *Description:* Also known as Chinese okra, silk squash, sze gwa and sing qua. A member of the gourd family, angled luffa looks like an English cucumber with ridges running the entire length, 1 - 2" in diameter and 10 - 24" in length. *Selection:* Dark green fruits with tender ridges. *Storage:* Refrigerate in plastic bag. *Preparation & use:* Remove ridges and peel away some of the skin, when cooked, the sweet, slightly spongy white flesh and the crispy green skin makes a very interesting contrast and a unique eating experience. Use in stir-fry or soup, alone or with other vegetables. *Availability*: Most of the year at Asian markets. *Substitute*: Smooth-skin luffa.

ASIAN CHILI OIL: *Description*: Also called red pepper oil or hot oil. Red colored oil made from hot red chili peppers and sesame and/or vegetable oil. Sold in bottles. *Storage*: Room temperature. *Availability*: Asian markets and many supermarkets. *Substitute*: Tabasco sauce.

ASIAN CHILI SAUCE *Description*: A thick, ketchup-like, red sauce made from fresh red hot chili peppers. There are many brands on the market. Try different brands to find the one best to your liking. *Storage*: Refrigerate after opening. *Availability*: Asian markets, Latin markets and many supermarkets. *Substitute*: Asian chili oil, Tabasco sauce, cayenne pepper or fresh chili peppers. *Do not substitute chili sauce from the ketchup section of the supermarket.*

ASIAN SESAME OIL: *Description*: An amber-colored oil made from toasted sesame seeds. Has a strong, rich, nutty, aroma and flavor. *Storage*: Room temperature. Good as long as it does not smell rancid. *Availability*: Asian markets and many supermarkets. *Substitute*: None. *Do not substitute sesame seed oil made from untoasted sesame seeds.*

BABY BOK CHOY: *Description*: A shorter version of regular bok choy, 6 - 8" in length. Has a finer texture and a sweeter taste than regular bok choy. See also BOK CHOY, REGULAR

BABY CORN, CANNED: *Description:* Miniature corn-on-the-cob packed in water, varies in length from 2 - 3". *Storage:* Unopened, at room temperature. Opened, unused corn should be immersed in cold water and refrigerate, change water daily, will keep up to 7 days. *Preparation & use*: Can be eaten as is from the can. Use in stir-fry, soup or salad. *Availability:* Asian markets and supermarkets. *Substitute*: None.

BAMBOO SHOOTS, CANNED: *Description:* Whole, half, chunk, tips; sliced or shredded, packed in water. Available in various size cans. *Storage:* Unopened, at room temperature. Opened, unused bamboo shoots should be immersed in cold water and refrigerate, change water daily, will keep up to 7 days. *Preparation & use:* Drain and rinse before using in stir-fry or salad. *If desired, blanch 10 seconds in boiling water, cool and drain, to remove any canned taste.*

Availability: Asian markets and supermarkets. **Substitute**: None.

BEAN SAUCE: ***Description:*** A thick, chutney-like, brown, salty paste made from soybeans packed in cans or bottles. Available in two forms: regular (some of the beans are left whole) and ground. **Storage**: Once opened, canned bean sauce should be transferred to a non-corrosive container with a tight fitting lid, date and label. Store bottled bean sauce in its original container. Refrigerate. ***Availability:*** Asian markets. **Substitute**: Miso.

BEAN SPROUTS: See MUNG BEAN SPROUTS and SOY BEAN SPROUTS.

BEAN THREADS: ***Description:*** Also know as fun sze, glass noodles and cellophane noodles. Threadlike, wiry, translucent noodles made from mung bean flour. Package sizes varies from 1.7 ounces to 1 pound. **Storage:** Room temperature. **Preparation & use**: Soak in water to soften also to make cutting into shorter lengths easier. If you must cut bean threads in its dry form, put them in a large plastic or paper bag (to prevent them from flying) and cut with a strong pair of scissors. ***Availability:*** Asian markets and some supermarkets. **Substitute**: None.

BITTER MELON: ***Description:*** Also known as balsam pear and foo gwa. Bitter melon looks like a cucumber with warts. Color range from white to emerald green, 1¼ - 2" in diameter and 4 -12" in length. **Storage**: 1. Place in a clean, dry paper bag. 2. Place in plastic bag. 3. Refrigerate. Will stay fresh 1 week or more. **Preparation & use**: Remove and discard seeds and pulp, do not peel. Use in stir-fry and soup. The bitter taste is prized by some, loathe by others (This is truly an acquired taste vegetable). Blanching or salting will remove some of the bitter taste. *To blanch: Simmer slices in boiling water 1 - 2 minutes, drain, cool, drain again. To salt: Toss slices with salt (1 teaspoon for each 2 cups). Let stand 10 - 15 minutes. Rinse and squeeze dry.* **Availability**: Year round in Asian markets. **Substitute**: None.

BLACK BEAN CAKE: See page 166.

BLACK BEANS, FERMENTED: See fermented black beans.

BLACK SESAME SEEDS; See SESAME SEEDS

BOK CHOY, REGULAR: ***Description***: Also spelled bak choi or baicai. A non-heading variety of Chinese cabbage 12" or more in length, with long, white, tender leaf stalks and green, oval leaves. **Selection**: Fresh-looking, unblemished plants. **Storage**: 1. Place in a clean, dry paper bag or wrap with dry paper towel. Place in perforated plastic bag. 3. Refrigerate. Will stay fresh 7-10 days. **Preparation & use**: Separate stalks, wash well. Discard yellowed and blemished parts. Use both stalks and leaves in stir-fry or soup. *A high water-content vegetable.* **Availability**: Year round in Asian markets and supermarkets. **Substitute**: Baby bok choy, Shanghai bok choy or napa cabbage.

BROWN RICE: See page 46.

BULL HEAD BARBECUE SAUCE: ***Description***: A thick, peanut butter-like brown seafood base sauce with a layer of oil on the surface. Sold in cans or jars. **Storage**: Unopened cans or jars at room temperature, opened cans or jars in the refrigerator. **Preparation & use**: Stir well before using. ***Availability:*** Asian markets. **Substitute**: Hoisin sauce.

CHAYOTE: ***Description***: Also known as mirliton. A 4 - 6" pear-shaped squash with pale green or white skin. **Selection**: Firm, heavy, unblemished ones. **Storage**: Refrigerate in plastic bag, will keep a week or more. **Preparation & use**: Cut in half lengthwise to remove and discard the seed (some people eat the seed). Peel and use as you would summer squash. *The juice from fresh peeled chayote will leave a gluelike film on your hands, will wash off eventually, wear gloves if this will bother you. Availability*: Year round in Asian markets, Latin markets and many supermarkets. *Substitute:* Chinese radish, summer squash or kohlrabi.

CHILI OIL, ASIAN: See ASIAN CHILI OIL

CHILI PEPPERS, FRESH: *Description*: Many varieties available. Sizes range from 1" or shorter to 4" or longer. Mild to very, very hot and size has no bearing on the heat. Color red, orange, yellow or green. Shape can be long and skinny, twisted or straight, or short and round. *Selection*: Firm, unblemished ones. *Storage*: Refrigerate in paper bag. Will keep 1 week or more. Freeze well. *Preparation & use*: Whole or minced. For less heat, remove and discard seeds and membrane. Do not touch eyes or other sensitive areas of the face when handling chili peppers. Wash hands immediately after handling or wear gloves if possible. *Substitute*: Asian chili sauce, Tabasco sauce, cayenne peppers or dried chilies.

CHILI SAUCE, ASIAN: See ASIAN CHILI SAUCE

CHINESE CHIVES: *Description:* Also known as garlic chives. Flat, bright green leaves ¼" wide and 6 - 9" long. Has a delicate garlic flavor. The flower stems, including buds, are also edible. *Selection*: Clean, fresh looking and uniformly green leaves. *Storage*: 1. Place in a clean, dry paper bag or wrap with dry paper towel. 2. Place in plastic bag. 3. Refrigerate. Will stay fresh 1 week or more. *Preparation & use*: Wash, trim and discard browned or bruised parts. Cut to desired lengths, cook and serve alone as a vegetable or combine with other vegetables. *Availability*: Asian markets. *Substitute*: Scallions or onion.

CHINESE EGGPLANT: *Description*: Long, slender with pale violet skin that is thin, tender and never needs peeling. Sweet, silky texture and few seeds. 6 - 12" in length. *Selection*: Pale violet, smooth, firm, unblemished ones that feels heavy for the size. *Storage*: Refrigerate in plastic bag. *Preparation & use*: Remove and discard calyx, cut to desired size and shape. *Makes great Eggplant Parmigiana. Substitute*: Japanese, Italian or regular eggplant.

CHINESE LONG BEANS: *Description*: Also known as yard-long beans. Varies in length from 12 - 36". There are two varieties: dark green and pale green. The dark green variety has a firm, crisp texture; the pale green variety has a softer, meatier texture. They are interchangeable. *Selection*: Firm beans with smooth pods and small seeds, avoid beans with rusty spots, feel spongy or hollow. *Storage*: 1. Place in a clean, dry paper bag or wrap with dry paper towel. 2. Place in plastic bag. 3. Refrigerate. Use within a few days. *Preparation & use*: Remove ends, cut to desired lengths, may be stir-fried, steamed, deep-fried or boiled. *Availability*: Asian markets. Best during the summer and fall. *Substitute*: String beans.

CHINESE MUSHROOMS: See DRIED CHINESE MUSHROOMS

CHINESE NOODLES: *Description*: Sold fresh or dried. The pale yellow noodles are made with wheat flour, eggs, water, salt and is dusted lightly with cornstarch. Available in various thickness - very fine to ¼". The most common is the 1/16" thickness (similar to number 8 spaghetti) and is labeled lo mein noodles by some manufacturers. The off white noodles are made without eggs and are labeled Shanghai noodles by some manufacturers. *Selection*: Fresh noodles should look and feel dry, with uniform color and no gray/green spots (indicate mold). *Storage*: Fresh, up to 5 days in refrigerator 3 months in freezer. Dried, at room temperature. *Preparation & use*: Follow package or recipe directions. *Availability*: Asian markets and many supermarkets. *Sub-*

stitute: Any kind of fresh or dried egg noodles or pasta.

CHINESE PANCAKES: *Description*: 8 - 10" thin pancakes made with flour and water. 10 - 12 pieces in a pack. *Preparation & use*: Thaw and use as is or thaw and steam for a softer, pliable texture. *Availability*: Frozen in Asian markets. *Substitute*: steamed pita or flour tortilla.

CHINESE PARSLEY: *Description*: Also known as cilantro or coriander. An herb, 6 - 9" long, with an aroma and flavor all its own. Has flat, thin, lacy green leaves and long thin stems. Usually sold with roots. *Selection*: Plants that are fresh with bright green bushy leaves. *Storage*: With roots attached: set in a glass of water and cover with an inflated plastic bag, will keep for 1 week. Without roots: place in an inflated plastic bag, will keep 2 - 3 days. *Preparation & use*: Use, both leaves and stems, as a vegetable or as an herb, fresh or cooked. In Southeast Asia, the roots are also used in cooking. *Availability*: Year round in Asian markets, Latin markets and supermarkets. *Substitute*: None.

CHINESE RADISH: *Description*: Also known as daikon. A long , white, carrot-shaped root vegetable that belongs to the same family as red radish. 1½ - 3" in diameter and 8 - 12" in length. Relatively mild, very crisp and has a high-water content. *Selection*: Roots that are heavy with smooth skin and no soft spots. *Storage*: Refrigerate in plastic bag. *Preparation & use*: Peel and use in stir-fry, soup and stew. Makes great pickle. *Availability*: Year round in Asian markets and many supermarkets. *Substitute*: Peeled icicle radish or peeled red radish.

CHINESE RED DATES: *Description*: Also known as jujubes. A sweet, dark-red, wrinkled, ready-to-eat dried fruit about the size of olive with a sharp pointed pit, also available pitted. Packed in plastic bags. *Selection*: Clean looking dried fruit. *Storage*: Room temperature. *Preparation & use*: In sweet or savory soups, braised and steamed dishes. Great out-of-bag snack food. *Availability*: Asian markets. *Substitute*: None.

CHINESE ROAST PORK: *Description*: A Cantonese specialty. Red colored, roasted marinated strips of pork that is a bit sweet. Sold by weight. *Storage*: Refrigerate. Freeze well. *Preparation & use*: Slice and eat as is or use in stir-fry with vegetables. Combine with other meat, poultry, seafood or tofu. *Availability*: Asian markets. *Substitute*: Any roast pork or ham.

CHINESE SAUSAGE: *Description*: These 6-inch long, ¾-inch in diameter, hard sausages are made from pork or liver. Pork sausage has a pinkish-red color, liver sausage has a dark reddish-brown color. Sold loose by the pair weighing about 2½ ounces, or by the pound in plastic bags. *Storage*: A month in the refrigerator, 3 months in freezer. *Preparation & use*: As you would bacon or pancetta. *Steam for 20 minutes or until the fat is soft and translucent, slice and serve as an appetizer or side dish.* *Availability*: Asian markets. *Substitute*: Pancetta, prosciutto or bacon.

CHINESE RED VINEGAR: *Description*: Red-colored vinegar packed in bottles. *Preparation & use*: Usually as a condiment. *Storage*: Room temperature. *Availability*: Asian markets. *Substitute*: Cider vinegar.

CHINESE ROCK SUGAR: *Description*: Irregularly shaped chunks of white to pale-gold sugar. Made from a combination of honey, maltose (sweetener made from barley) and raw sugar, sold in 1 pound plastic bag or in box. *Storage*: Room temperature. *Preparation & use*: Use a hammer or nut cracker to break into smaller pieces. *Do not pulverize in the food processor.* Frequently used in braising to give finished dish a glaze and gravy a rich flavor. Also used to sweeten tea. *Availability*: Asian market. *Substitute*: Any kind of sugar or honey.

CHINKIANG VINEGAR: **Description**: Also known as brown vinegar. Actually more black than brown. Made from glutinous rice, it has a sweet fragrance and tart, distinctive flavor. Packed in bottle. **Storage**: Room temperature. **Availability & use**: Asian markets. **Substitute**: Balsamic vinegar.

CHOY SUM: **Description**: Also referred to as Chinese flowering cabbage and Chinese broccoli raab. A member of the cabbage family with bright green leaves, yellow flowers and stalks ¼ - ½" in diameter and 6 - 8" long. **Selection**: Bright green unblemished leaves and firm stalks. Avoid any with soft, spongy or white spot in the middle of the stalk. **Storage**: 1. Place in clean, dry paper bag or wrap with dry paper towel. 2. Place in a plastic bag. 3. Refrigerate. Will stay fresh up to 1 week. **Preparation & use**: Wash well. Use all parts (stems, leaves and flowers), leave whole or cut into shorter lengths, in stir-fry or in soup, alone or in combination with other vegetables. Considered by many as the best of the Chinese cabbages. **Availability**: Most of the year in Asian markets. **Substitute**: Broccoli rabe.

CILANTRO: See CHINESE PARSLEY

CLOUD EARS: **Description**: Also known as tree ears, a fungus that grows on tree, irregularly shaped (look like bits of crumbled paper), about ½" pieces, black on one side, a shade lighter on the other side and about the thickness of thumbnail. (Not to be confused with wood ears, a cousin, which are much larger and thicker, black on one side and near white and fuzzy on the other.) After soaking, swell to 2 - 3 times its dry form. Has a crunchy and slightly rubbery texture. Sold in plastic bags of varying weights. **Storage**: Room temperature. **Preparation & use**: Soak in lots of water to soften and bloom, 15 - 30 minutes. Remove and discard any attached woody and sandy bits or soft gelatinous parts. Rinse and drain. Cover with cold water and refrigerate until ready to use. Drain before using. The black, crunchy, rubbery ingredient in Hot & Sour Soup and Mu Shu dishes is cloud ears. **Availability**: Asian markets and specialty food stores. **Substitute**: Chinese dried mushrooms.

COCONUT MILK, UNSWEETENED: **Description**: Creamy liquid extracted from grated fresh coconut flesh. Sold in cans. **Storage**: Unopened can at room temperature. Opened unused portion up to 3 days in refrigerator. **Availability**: Asian markets and many supermarkets. (Read the label, there is also canned sweetened coconut milk. Do not use as a substitute.) **Substitute**: In a blender, blend 1 cup desiccated coconut combined with 2¾ cups very hot water and a pinch of salt for about 25 seconds. Strain through a cheesecloth-line strainer, pressing and squeezing out all the liquid. Discard pulp.

COCONUT ROLLS: See page 167.

CREAMY-CHINESE STYLE DRIED NOODLES: **Description**: 8" long strips of dried noodles, sold in 12 - 16 ounce packages, similar in thickness to linguine. **Storage**: Room temperature. **Preparation & use**: Cook in lots of boiling water until al dente, drain and cool under running water. Drain again thoroughly. **Availability**: Asian markets. **Substitute**: Linguine.

CURRY POWDER: **Description**: A golden yellow blend of different ground spices. Typical ingredients are: coriander seeds, cumin, chilies, tumeric, cinnamon and ginger. **Storage**: Tightly covered away from heat, light and moisture. **Availability**: Asian markets and supermarkets. **Substitute**: None.

DARK SOY SAUCE: **Description**: A salty, dark liquid made from soy beans and wheat. Because it contains molasses, dark soy sauce is darker, slightly thicker and a little sweeter than regular soy sauce. **Selection**: Shake the bottle. If a dark coating remains on the inside of the bottle, it is dark soy sauce. **Preparation & use**: Gives food a dark rich color and robust flavor. Use in place of regular soy sauce if on a sodium-restricted diet but want a soy flavor and color. Substitute: 1 - 2 teaspoons dark (or mushroom) soy sauce for 3 teaspoons of regular soy sauce. **Storage**: Room temperature unless label on bottle states otherwise. **Availability**: Asian markets. **Substitute**: Mushroom soy sauce. See also REGULAR SOY SAUCE.

DEEP FRIED TOFU: See page 74

DRIED BEAN CURD: See page 74.

DRIED CHINESE MUSHROOMS,: **Description**: Also known as doong goo, black mushrooms or shiitake mushrooms. There are two varieties available in Asian markets. The most common and least expensive variety, *hsiang goo* (fragrant mushroom), has black caps and tan gills, is sold, with or without stems, loose or in plastic bags. The other variety, *hwa goo* (flower mushroom), has a patterned cap, with tan fissures running through a dark background. After soaking, hwa goo nearly doubles in thickness. Cooked hwa goo has a plush, chewy texture that is very satisfying. Hwa goo requires a longer soaking period than hsiang goo. Sold loose, in plastic bags or packaged in fancy box for gift giving. Size and pattern determines the cost. Both are interchangeable. **Selection**: Dry, clean looking and fragrant. **Storage**: At room temperature, in an airtight container with a few bay leaves. (Make sure mushrooms are thoroughly dry before storing, if in doubt, spread on paper towel and air dry) **Preparation and use**: Soak in water to soften (If time permits choose cold water, takes longer to soften, over warm water. OK to soak overnight in the refrigerator.) Remove and discard stems (or save stems, after redrying, to flavor broth). Use as per recipe. For mincing purposes, the less expensive kind will do. For thick slices or for serving whole I go for hwa goo. **Availability**: Asian markets, specialty food markets and supermarkets. **Substitute**: Fresh shiitake mushrooms or other fresh mushrooms. If chopped to use as part of a filling, saute to get rid of some of the excess moisture.

DRIED LOTUS ROOT: **Description**: Round or oval, about ⅜" thick, tan color, holey disks package in plastic bags. **Storage**: Room temperature in an airtight container with a couple bay leaves. **Preparation**: If using in soup, rinse and add to pot with other ingredients. If using in stir-fry, soak in warm water for 2 hours or more. Slice thinly, crosswise. Immerse in cold water until ready to use. Drain before using. **Availability**: Asian markets. **Substitute**: Fresh lotus root. See also LOTUS ROOT.

DRIED RICE CAKE: **Description**: Made from rice flour. They look like miniature white tongue depressors. Sold in 8 - 16 ounce plastic bags. **Storage**: Room temperature. **Preparation & use**: Soak before using. Cooked rice cake has a pleasant chewy texture. **Availability**: Asian markets. **Substitute**: None.

DRIED SCALLOPS: **Description**: These golden to light brown nuggets are delicious and expensive. Come in various sizes ranging from ½-inch diameter to more than an inch. The larger the dried scallops the higher the price. **Selection**: Whole scallops should be cleaning looking, if purchasing broken pieces there should be no dregs. **Storage**: In an airtight container at room temperature or in the freezer. **Preparation & use**: If used in soup, stew or congee to enhance flavor, rinse and add to pot with other ingredients. If using in stir-fry or gravy, rinse then soak in water to soften, rub with fingers to separate fibers, use as recipe directed, soaking liquid is used as well. To retain the natural flavor of dried scallops, refrain from adding soy sauce or oyster sauce to the recipe. **Availability**: Asian markets and Chinese pharmacies. **Substitute**: None.

EGG CUSTARD: See page 166.

FERMENTED BEAN CURD: **Description**: Also known as fermented tofu and Chinese cheese. About 1" white cubes of tofu (bean curd) that went through a fermentation process and is preserved in brine. It has a creamy texture and a cheesy taste. Packed in bottles, available plain or with hot chili flakes. **Storage**: Refrigerate after opening. **Preparation & use**: As is as a condiment or in cooking to flavor vegetables. **Availability**: Asian markets. **Substitute**: None. *Not to be confused with red bean curd which is also a type of fermented tofu cubes. See RED BEAN CURD.*

FERMENTED BLACK BEANS: **Description**: Also called salted black beans or preserved beans. These dry, soft, salty beans are made from black soybeans and taste like dried-cured olives. Some have ginger slices added and others are seasoned with five-spice powder. Packaged in plastic bag or cardboard container. **Storage**: Room temperature in an airtight non-corrosive container. **Preparation & use**: To rinse or not to rinse before using is strictly a personal preference. Frequently paired with minced garlic and fresh ginger to flavor meat, poultry and vegetables. **Availability**: Asian markets and specialty food markets. **Substitute**: None.

FISH SAUCE: **Description**: A dark colored sauce made from fish extract. Looks like soy sauce. Packed in bottle. **Storage**: Room temperature unless stated otherwise on bottle. **Preparation & use**: As you would regular soy sauce. **Availability**: Asian markets and specialty food markets. **Substitute**: Regular soy sauce.

FIVE-SPICE POWDER: **Description**: A brown spice made from a blend of star anise, cloves, Szechuan (Sichuan) peppercorns, fennel and Chinese cinnamon. **Storage**: In an airtight container, preferably glass, at room temperature, away from heat, light and moisture, Good as long as it retains its aroma. **Preparation & use**: Sparingly to season and flavor food. **Availability**: Asian markets, specialty food markets and some supermarkets. **Substitute**: A combination of the above mentioned spiced to suit own taste.

FIVE-SPICE PRESSED TOFU: See page 74.

FROZEN TOFU: See page 74

FUN WON ROLLS: See page 167.

FUZZY MELON: **Description**: Looks like a chubby cucumber covered with white stubble. A member of the wintermelon family, fuzzy melon could be called Chinese summer squash as it is used in much the same manner as Western summer squash. **Selection**: Small green fuzzy melons that are heavy, firm and blemish free. **Storage**: 1. Place in a clean, dry brown paper bag or wrap with paper towels. 2. Put into a perforated plastic bag. 3. Refrigerate. Will keep up to 2 weeks. **Preparation & use**: Peel, slice or cube, use in stir-fry, soup or stew, no need to remove seeds. **Substitute**: Summer squash.

GAI LAN: **Description**: Also known as Chinese broccoli. A member of the cabbage family. A leafy vegetable with white flowers and smooth fat stalks ½ ¾" in diameter and 8 10" in length.. **Selection**: Thick stalks with green, waxy, unblemished leaves and more of the white flowers in bud than in bloom. Avoid ones with white spot in the middle of the stalks. **Storage**: Refrigerate in plastic bags. Will keep a week. **Preparation & use**: Cook whole, cut into short sections or cook sliced leaves and stems separately. Peel root end of stalk if appears fibrous. **Availability**: Most of the year in Asian markets. **Substitute**: Broccoli.

GINGER: **Description**: A knobby, beige-brown rhizome with thin dry skin. Fresh ginger can be purchased in two forms: young and mature. Young ginger (not available all year) has a thin translucent pinkish-yellow skin. It is tender and fiber-free with a mild flavor. Mature ginger has a yellowish-brown skin. It is fibrous with a more pungent flavor. **Selection**: Young ginger with pink buds and smooth skin. Mature ginger with smooth, unwrinkled skin. **Storage**: At room temperature, in the refrigerator, in the freezer or immersed in pale dry sherry or Chinese rice wine. See page 16, *Ginger Wine*. **Preparation & use**: Young ginger, when available is used as a vegetable in stir-fry. *A popular Cantonese dish is stir-fry peeled and thinly sliced fresh young ginger with beef.* Mature ginger, use peeled or unpeeled; sliced, minced or crushed; to enhance the flavor of stir-fry, soups, stews. **Availability**: Asian markets, Latin markets and supermarkets. **Substitute**: None. *Do not use ground ginger as a substitute for fresh ginger.*

GINGKO NUTS: **Description**: Has a hard brownish-yellow smooth shell. The kernel inside is covered with a thin light brown skin. Remove the skin to reveal a soft cream color nut. **Selection**: Clean looking shells free from mold and discoloration. **Storage**: Refrigerate or freeze for longer storage. **Preparation & use**: Crack shell with a nut cracker, flat of a cleaver or the heel of your hand. Discard shell. Cover kernels with boiling water. Let stand 30 minutes. Slip off light brown skin. Use nuts in sweet or savory soups or in stir-fry with other ingredients. **Availability**: When in season in Asian markets. **Substitute**: Canned gingko nuts.

GLUTINOUS RICE: See page 46.

GREEN SOY BEANS: **Description**: Also known as green vegetable soy beans, edible soy beans and edamame. These are soy beans harvested at the green stage. Available shelled and unshelled. **Storage**: Keep frozen until ready to use. **Preparation & use**: Thaw and use shelled green soy beans as you would green peas. Unshelled, thaw, shell and use. Or boil frozen unshelled green soy beans in lightly salted water for 5 minutes. Serve as a snack, hot or at room temperature. **Availability**: Year round, in the frozen food section of Asian markets, health food stores and some supermarkets. **Substitute**: Green peas or lima beans.

HO FUN: **Description**: Made with rice flour and water. Available fresh or dried. Fresh ho fun comes in a thin folded sheet weighing about 1 pound. Dried ho fun is precut in widths about ¼" and wider. **Storage**: Fresh for up to 5 days in the refrigerator. May freeze, but tends to fall apart in cooking. Dried ho fun at room temperature. **Preparation & use**: Cut fresh ho fun to desired length and width before using. Soften by plunging into boiling water briefly, by steaming or in the microwave 2 - 3 minutes. Soak dried ho fun in cold water for 30 minutes, drain and use, or simmer in boiling water for 5 minutes until translucent. Drain and rinse in clod water. **Substitute**: None.

HOISIN SAUCE: **Description**: A thick (thicker than ketchup), dark, brownish-red soybean-based sauce with a slightly sweet and spicy taste. Packed in cans or jars. **Selection**: Many brands available, try different brands to find the one best to your liking. I like the Koon Chun brand. **Storage**: Once opened, canned hoisin sauce should be transferred to a non-corrosive container with a tight-fitting lid, date and label. Store bottled hoisin sauce in its original container. Refrigerate. **Availability**: Asian markets, specialty food stores and many supermarkets. **Substitute**: Bull Head Barbecue Sauce.

HONG KONG-STYLE PAN FRIED NOODLES: See page 59.

JA CHOY: **Description**: Also know as Szechuan (Sichuan) preserved vegetables. The knobby root end of a member of the cabbage family preserved with chili powder, salt and spices. Light green or light tan and covered with red chili paste. Crunchy, a bit salty and spicy, tastes like spicy sauerkraut. *Selection*: Packed in cans, shredded or whole. Whole ones are sold loose in some markets in Chinatown. *Storage*: Unopened cans at room temperature. Opened, unused portions should be transferred to a noncorrosive container with a tight fitting lid, date, label and refrigerate. *Preparation & use*: Shredded, rinse and use as is as a condiment, add to soup or stir-fry. Unshredded, rinse, slice or shred as desired. *Substitute*: Sauerkraut and chili peppers.

JASMINE RICE: See page 46.

JICAMA: *Description*: Also known as yam bean. A tuber that looks like a big turnip with sandy-brown skin. *Selection*: Smooth skin, firm, heavy and unblemished. *Storage*: Room temperature for 1 or 2 days, unwrapped in the refrigerate for up to 2 weeks. *Preparation & use*: Peel away the skin and any fibrous layer. The white flesh is crispy and sweet. Use cooked or uncooked. Frequently used as a substitute for water chestnuts in stir-fry. Great in salad. *Availability*: Asian markets, Latin markets and many supermarkets. *Substitute*: Water chestnuts.

KOHLRABI: *Description*: A swollen stem that looks like a turnip with leaves. Skin ranges from light green to purplish. The light green variety is more commonly seen in stores. *Selection*: kohlrabi that is smaller than a tennis ball. The larger ones tend to be woody. Leaves should be green and fresh looking. *Storage*: Refrigerate in plastic bag up to a week. *Preparation & use*: Peel, slice, cube or shred. Use in stir-fry, stew, salad or soup. *Availability*: Year round in Asian markets and supermarkets, but best during the summer and fall months. *Substitute*: Broccoli stem.

LAVER: *Description*: Also known as nori. A 7 x 8" dried thin rectangle sheet of dark purple-green edible seaweed. Sold in package of 10 - 12 sheets, toasted or untoasted. The dark thin wrapping used in making sushi is toasted nori. *Storage*: Room temperature. *Availability*: Asian markets and speciality markets. *Substitute*: None.

LICHEE: See page 167

LO MEIN NOODLES: See Noodles.

LONGAN: See page 168.

LOQUAT: See page 168.

LOTUS ROOT: *Description*: A tan rhizome that grows underwater and looks like links of very fat sausages. Cut away the nodes at the ends of each section to reveal tunnels that run the entire length of the section. *Selection*: Hard, whole unblemished roots, free of soft spots and with smooth, unblemished skin. *Storage*: Refrigerate in plastic bag with the corners cut away and the opened-end wide open. *Preparation & use*: Peel. Cut into slices or chunks. Use in stir-fry, soup or pickle. Thin cross-sections with their holey, lace-like patterns add elegance to any dish and are frequently used as a garnish. (Lotus root is very hard, to avoid cutting oneself, use a sharp knife.) *Availability*: July to February in Asian markets. *Substitute*: Dried or canned lotus root. *Virtually every part of the lotus plant is used. The leaves are used as a wrapper for steamed food; the seeds are used whole in soup (sweet or savory) and stews or puréed and sweetened to make filling for pastries; the seed pods are used in dried flower arrangements. The lotus flower, depicted widely in Chinese artwork is admired by the Chinese not only for its beauty but also as a symbol of the rebirth of humankind.*

LOTUS SEED CAKE: See page 166

MELON CAKE: See page 166.

MIRIM: ***Description***: Sweetened Japanese rice wine made from glutinous rice. Pale yellow liquid packed in glass or plastic bottle. ***Storage***: Room temperature. ***Availability***: Asian markets and specialty food markets. ***Substitute***: Sake, Chinese rice wine, or pale dry sherry with sugar added.

MISO: ***Description***: One of the basic ingredients in Japanese cuisine is a jam-like paste made from fermented soybeans. Color range from tan to dark brown. Packed in plastic bag or plastic container. ***Selection***: Because of the variations in color, taste and texture, try different variety to find the one best to your liking. For recipes in this book, I use the light brown miso. ***Storage***: Refrigerate. ***Availability***: Refrigeration section of Asian markets and health food stores. ***Substitute***: Ground Chinese bean sauce.

MOON CAKE: See page 166.

MUNG BEAN SPROUTS: ***Description***: Grown from mung beans, these are 2 - 3" long, clean-looking, crisp, white stem, with threadlike roots, attached to a ¼" long bean, sometimes with tiny leaf emerging and the green bean hull still clinging to it. ***Selection***: Short fat, (more tender than the long skinny ones) crisp, clean, white ones with firm beans. Avoid soft mushy ones. ***Storage***: Highly perishable. Refrigerate in plastic bag use within 1 - 2 days. ***Preparation & use***: Wash, discard any floating green hulls and yellowish sprouts. A high water-content vegetable, drain thoroughly before using in stir-fry. ***Availability***: Asian markets and supermarkets, loose or pre-packaged. ***Substitute***: Shredded (lengthwise) napa cabbage stems.

MUSHROOM SOY SAUCE: ***Description***: Dark soy sauce flavored with mushrooms. See also DARK SOY SAUCE and REGULAR SOY SAUCE.

NAPA CABBAGE: ***Description***: A heading variety of Chinese cabbage. Short, fat cabbage with wide stems and broad thin leaves. Milder and more tender than regular green cabbage, but with a higher water content. Selection: Heads that are white, fresh-looking, firm, heavy and free of soft spots. ***Storage***: 1. Put in a clean, dry paper bag or wrap in paper towels. 2. Place in plastic bag with the 2 corners cut away. 3. Refrigerate. Will keep 2 weeks or more. ***Preparation & use***: Remove and discard wilted and browned leaves. Wash outer leaves. Not necessary to wash inner leaves. Use in stir-fry, soup, pickle or salad. ***Availability***: Year round in Asian markets and supermarkets. ***Substitute***: Green cabbage, savoy cabbage or bok choy.

NOODLE CAKE: See page 166.

NOODLES, CHINESE EGG: See CHINESE NOODLES.

ONG CHOI: ***Description***: Also known as water spinach, has jointed hollow stem and pointed leaves. Two varieties available. A light green variety with wide arrowhead-shaped leaves and a dark green variety with long narrow pointed leaves. The light green variety has a crisp-tender texture, the dark green variety has a chewier texture. ***Selection***: Tender stems and green leaves. ***Storage***: Highly perishable. Refrigerate in plastic bag, using within 2 - 3 days. ***Preparation & use***: Wash and drain thoroughly. Break between jointed-stems. Stir-fry. Will shrink to ⅓ original volume. ***Substitute***: Spinach or Swiss chard.

OYSTER SAUCE: ***Description***: A salty, brown sauce made from oyster extract and spices. Sold in bottles or cans. Buy the top quality. To determine if you are getting the top quality, read the label, the first ingredient should be *oyster extractive*. ***Storage***: Unopened at room temperature.

Opened, bottled oyster sauce should be kept in its original container, canned oyster sauce should be transferred to a non-corrosive container with a tight-fitting lid, date and label. Refrigerate. *Availability*: Asian markets and some supermarkets. *Substitute*: Regular soy sauce.

PINE NUTS: *Description*: Also known as pignolo, pignon, pignolia or pinocchio nuts. The seeds from the cones of Roman or stone pine. Pine nuts are sold already shelled. They look like white corn kernel and about the same size. *Storage*: Because of the unstable resinous oils they contain, pine nuts become rancid very easily. Use as soon as purchased. For longer storage, keep in the freezer. *Preparation & use*: As is or roast at 300° until lightly browned. *Availability*: Asian markets, Italian markets and specialty food markets. *Substitute*: Any kind of nuts.

PRESERVED EGG: *Description*: Also known as pidan is duck egg cured in lime, ash and salt. At the end of the curing period, the egg white is transformed into a gelatinous texture that is gray-black and translucent. The yolk becomes semi-solid with a grayish-green color. Sold single or in pack of 6. *Storage*: Room temperature. *Preparation & use*: Shell, slice and serve as an appetizer (This is an acquired taste food.) accompanied with pickled young ginger, onion or shallots. Frequently used in congee. *Availability*: Asian markets. *Substitute*: None.

PRESERVED PLUMS: See page 142.

RED BEAN CURD: *Description*: Also called preserved bean curd. About 1" cubes of fermented bean curd (tofu) preserved in brine with rice wine and red rice added. The moist, creamy texture and pungent aroma of red bean curd is like that of a strong soft cheese. Sold in jars or crocks. *Storage*: Unopened, room temperature. Refrigerate after opening. *Preparation & use:* As a flavoring for meats. *Availability*: Asian markets. *Substitute*: None.

RED VINEGAR: See CHINESE RED VINEGAR.

REGULAR SOY SAUCE: *Description*: A salty dark liquid made from soybeans and wheat. (If you are allergic to wheat, use wheat-free tamari.) Packed in various size bottles. *Selection*: The sodium content of different brands of soy sauce will vary. *Read the label.* There will also be some taste variations among the many different brands on the market. Try different brands to find the one best to your liking. The recipes in this book were tested using naturally brewed Chinese soy sauce. *Storage*: Room temperature unless label on bottle states otherwise. *Availability*: Asian markets, specialty food markets and supermarkets. *Substitute*: Tamari.

RICE: See page 46.

RICE CAKE: See DRIED RICE CAKE

RICE NOODLES: See HO FUN and RICE STICKS

RICE STICKS: *Description*: Also called mee fun and rice vermicelli made from rice flour. Wire-thin opaque noodles that are quite brittle and turn white after soaking. *Storage*: Room temperature. *Preparation & use*: Soak in water to soften before using. *Availability*: Asian markets and supermarkets. *Substitute*: Dried ho fun.

RICE VINEGAR: *Description*: Actually all Chinese vinegars are made from rice. When a recipe calls for rice vinegar, it usually refers to the light yellow or white rice vinegar. Packed in bottles. *Storage*: Room temperature. *Availability*: Asian markets and supermarkets. *Substitute*: Regular white vinegar but use less than is called for in the recipe. The acidity level in rice vinegar tends to be lower than white vinegar, check the label.

SALTED BLACK BEANS: See FERMENTED BLACK BEANS

SESAME RICE DUMPLING: See page 166.

SESAME SEED PASTE, ASIAN: *Description*: A thick (peanut butter consistency), dark brown paste with sesame oil floating on top. Made from toasted sesame seeds. *Storage*: Refrigerate after opening. *Preparation & use*: Stir to incorporate. *Availability*: Asian markets, specialty food markets and some supermarkets. *Substitute*: Peanut butter. *Do not use tahini (sesame seed paste, made from untoasted sesame seed, used in Middle Eastern cuisine) as a substitute.*

SESAME SEEDS: *Description*: Can be either black or white. There is no difference in taste between the two which are interchangeable in cooking. White sesame seeds are available hulled or unhulled. *Storage*: In the freezer, date and label. Will keep up to 2 years. *Preparation & use*: Roast before using to bring out the flavor. See page 165. *Availability*: Asian markets, health food stores, specialty food markets and supermarkets. *Substitute*: Any roasted seeds and nuts.

SHALLOTS: *Description*: A member of the onion family. Look like clumps of petite onions with reddish-brown skin. *Selection*: Firm clean heads. *Storage*: Room temperature. *Preparation & use*: Peel. Use as you would onion. Can be eaten raw or cooked. *Availability*: Year round in Asian markets and supermarkets. *Substitute*: White part of scallion or onion.

SHANGHAI BOK CHOY: *Description*: Similar to baby bok choy, except the leaf stalks are pale green with a bulbous base. More delicate in taste and texture than baby bok choy. See also BABY BOK CHOY and BOK CHOY, REGULAR

SHIITAKE MUSHROOMS: See DRIED CHINESE MUSHROOMS

SICHUAN PEPPERCORNS: *Description*: Also called flower pepper. Reddish-brown, open pods with tiny black seeds mixed in. Mildly spicy, the pods have a slight numbing effect on the tongue when chewed. *Selection*: Bags with more pods than seeds. *Storage*: In an airtight container, away from heat, light and moisture. Good as long as it retains its aroma. *Availability*: Asian markets. *Substitute*: Peppercorns.

SILK SQUASH: See Angled luffa

SNOW PEAS: *Description*: Also called Chinese pea pods. Flat green pod, about ½" wide and about 2½" long enclosing small immature peas. *Selection*: Green, unblemished pods with small peas inside, that are crisp and fresh-looking. *Storage*: 1. Place in a clean, dry paper bag. 2. Place bag in a plastic bag. 3. Refrigerate. Will keep up to 1 week or more. *Preparation*: Snap the stem end toward the peas side. Pull the string along the pea side. String the other side, if desired. The whole pod is eaten. Use in stir-fry, soup or salad. Availability: Year round in Asian markets and supermarkets. *Substitute*: Sugar snap peas.

SOY BEAN SPROUTS: *Description*: Grown from dried soy beans, soy beans sprouts are high in protein. 2½ - 3" long whitish stem attached to a ¾" pale yellow bean. *Selection*: Fresh, clean, firm sprouts. Avoid any with emerging leaves and brown/black or soft beans. *Storage*: Refrigerate in plastic bags. Use within a few days. *Preparation*: Trim away root ends. Wash and drain well. Use whole or chop coarsely. *Availability*: Asian markets and some supermarkets. *Substitute*: None.

SOY SAUCE: See REGULAR SOY SAUCE, DARK SOY SAUCE and MUSHROOM SOY SAUCE

SPONGE CAKE, BROWN: See page 167

SPONGE CAKE, WHITE: See page 167.

SPRING ROLL SKIN: *Description*: Also known as Shanghai egg roll skin and Chinese pastry wafer. Made from flour, these off-white, thin, wafer-like crepes are available, 8 - 10"-round or 8"-square, 10 - 25 to a pack. *Selection*: No dry or broken edges. *Storage*: Freeze up to 3 months. *Preparation & use*: Thaw in refrigerator. Keep unused sheets covered with plastic while making rolls to prevent drying out. Cover completed rolls with plastic or wax paper if not frying at once. *Availability*: Freezer section of Asian markets. *Substitute*: Egg roll skin.

STAR ANISE: *Description*: An eight point star-shaped brown pod with a shiny brown seed in each point. Has a licorice-like flavor. *Selection*: Clean looking pods with strong aroma. *Storage*: At room temperature in an air-tight container away from light, heat and moisture. Good as long as it retains its aroma. *Preparation & use*: Use sparingly whole pod or crushed. *Availability*: Asian markets and specialty food markets. *Substitute*: None.

STRAW MUSHROOMS, CANNED: *Description*: There are two kinds of canned straw mushrooms: peeled and unpeeled. Unpeeled straw mushrooms look like quail eggs. If not harvested at this stage, the cap will break through the membrane resulting in peeled straw mushrooms that look like a closed, short, fat umbrella. Peeled and unpeeled straw mushrooms are interchangeable. *Selection*: Both are available in small, medium or large size. Unpeeled straw mushrooms cost more than peeled. *Storage*: Unopened can at room temperature, immerse opened unused portions in water and refrigerate. Change water daily. Will keep up to 3 days. *Preparation & use*: Drain and rinse. Leave whole or cut in halves. *Availability*: Asian markets and supermarkets. *Substitute*: Fresh mushrooms.

SUGAR SNAP PEAS: *Description*: Look like regular green peas but the pods are edible. See SNOW PEAS.

SZE GWA: See ANGLED LUFFA

SZECHUAN PEPPERCORNS: See SICHUAN PEPPERCORNS

SZECHUAN PRESERVED VEGETABLES: See JA CHOY

TAPIOCA STARCH: *Description*: Looks like cornstarch, it is made from cassava root. Packed in paper covered with plastic wrapping. *Storage*: Room temperature. *Preparation & use*: Dissolve in water before using. *Availability*: Asian markets. *Substitute*: Cornstarch or potato starch

TARO ROOT: *Description*: The large main corm also known as dasheen, looks like a barrel-shaped rutabaga and can weigh 1½ pounds and more. The small subsidiary corm (was attached to the main corm) known as eddo, looks like a small Idaho potato. Both large and small corm have brown hairy skin encircled with rings. The starchy flesh range in color from white, pink and purple and has a delicate nutty flavor. The famous Hawaiian poi is made from taro. *Selection*: Firm, heavy roots with no soft spots. *Storage*: Room temperature. *Preparation & use*: Peel. Use much in the same manner as potato. *Some people may be allergic to the oxalate crystals in raw taro (cause itchy skin) if so, wear gloves when peeling*. *Availability*: Year round in Asian markets, Latin markets and many supermarkets. *Substitute*: Potato.

TIANJIN BEAN SHEET: *Description*: Also known as Tianjin green bean starch sheet. 11" diameter, thin, transparent circle made from mung beans (green bean) starch. *Storage*: Room temperature. *Preparation & use*: Soak in boiling water before cutting into desired length and width. *Availability*: Asian markets. *Substitute*: Bean threads.

TIGER LILY FLOWERS: **Description**: Also called golden needles, the dried unopened buds of the tiger lily plant. About 3" long and look like, pliable, gold-brown hay. **Storage**: Room temperature. **Preparation & use**: Soak in warm water to soften. Remove and discard any hard woody parts. **Availability**: Asian markets and specialty food markets. **Substitute**: None.

TOFU: See page 72.

TOFU, DEEP FRIED: See page 73.

TOFU, 5-SPICED PRESSED: See page 74.

TOFU, FROZEN: See page 74.

TOFU, SHREDDED PRESSED, See page 74.

WATER CHESTNUT: **Description**: A small, round, 1 - 1½" in diameter, edible root, with a pointed top and brown-black skin and white flesh. Canned water chestnuts are used in this book. **Selection**: Fresh - firm with no soft spots. Canned - available sliced or whole. **Storage**: Fresh - refrigerate in plastic bags. Canned - unopened, at room temperature, opened, unused portion refrigerate. **Preparation & use**: Fresh - Wash and peel. The white flesh is sweet and crunchy. Can be eaten raw or used in cooking. Canned - open, drain and rinse. **Availability**: Fresh - seasonal, in Asian markets. Canned - Asian markets and supermarkets. **Substitute**: Jicama.

WATERCRESS: **Description**: A mildly pungent vegetable with small irregular-size dark green leaves and a slight curvy, hollow stem, 6 - 8" in length. **Selection**: Sold by the bunch. **Storage**: Refrigerate in plastic bag. **Preparation & use**: Wash thoroughly. Discard wilted, bruised or yellowed parts. Leave whole or cut into shorter lengths. Stir-fry or in soup. **Availability**: Asian markets and supermarkets. **Substitute**: None.

WINTERMELON: **Description**: Belonging to the gourd family, mature wintermelon has a hard green skin covered with a dusting of white powder and stubbles and can weigh anywhere from 5 pounds and up to 35 pounds. **Selection**: Commonly sold by the slice, should have plump firm white flesh with a clean smell. **Storage**: Place in a clean day paper bag. The cut area will dry out a bit, but stored this way the piece will keep 2 weeks or more. *This is a very high water content item, stored in plastic bag it will spoil very quickly. You do not want it to rot in your refrigerator. The smell is not pleasant.* **Preparation & use**: Remove and discard seed and spongy pulp. Peel, cut white flesh to desired size. Used mostly in soup. **Substitute**: Fuzzy melon or zucchini.

WONTON WRAPPERS: **Description**: Also called wonton skin. A 3½" square egg-noodle dough made with wheat flour, egg and water. Fresh wrappers are smooth, pliable and easy to work with. Sold in 1 pound packages wrapped in moisture-proof paper or plastic. *Wonton wrappers are great for making ravioli.* **Selection**: Fresh looking with no dried or split edges. Wonton wrappers sold in Asian markets come in various thicknesses. The one I prefer is labeled "thin wonton skin" and has about 90 wrappers to a pound. The ones sold in supermarkets are much thicker. **Storage**: Refrigerate up to one week. Freeze up to 3 months. **Preparation & use**: Cover unused wrappers and completed wontons with a clean, damp kitchen towel to prevent drying out. If wrappers are frozen, thaw in refrigerator before using. **Availability**: Refrigeration section of Asian markets and supermarkets. **Substitute**: None

INDEX

COOKBOOKS ORDER FORM _Good Value Gift – Holidays, birthdays!_

Date _____

Person placing order (please print): **Name** _____

Address _____

_____

Personalized To (please print) _____
(A personalized cookbook makes a unique gift that is inexpensive, valuable and will last a lifetime.)

MY STUDENTS' FAVORITE CHINESE RECIPES, updated edition ...... US$14.00 x _____ = _____
(A collection of classroom-tested popular recipes)

WOKKING YOUR WAY TO LOW FAT COOKING................US$12.50 x _____ = _____
(A collection of classroom-tested low-fat high-flavor recipes)

SUB-TOTAL _____

NYS residents add applicable sales tax ...... _____

TOTAL DUE _____

Please send completed form with check payable to: **Norma Chang**
P.O. Box 911
Wappingers Falls, NY 12590
(cookbooks are also available through Amazon.com)

CREATE A GIFT WOK OR A GIFT BASKET

Line a wok or a basket with kitchen towel or crumbled tissue paper.

Arrange in wok/basket:
Norma Chang's cookbook/s
Homemade ginger wine
(recipe in Norma Chang's cookbooks)

Add to wok/basket a selection of the following:
1 bottle of mushroom and/or dark soy sauce
1 bottle of regular soy sauce
1 bottle of hoisin sauce
1 jar of Asian chili sauce
1 bottle of Asian sesame oil
A bag of black sesame seeds
A bag of star anise
A bag of 5-spice powder
Chinese tea

For your gardening friends, add to wok/basket:
garden catalog
packets of Chinese vegetable seeds

Wrap wok/basket with cellophane paper and tie with a pretty ribbon.